Foreclosure Defense: Litigation Strategies and Appeals

Kimberly Alderman, JD

ERLEICHDA

Published by Erleichda Press

LIBRARY OF CONGRESS CATALOGUING IN
PUBLICATION DATA
Alderman, Kimberly
Foreclosure Defense: Litigation Strategies and Appeals
p. cm.

ISBN 978-0-9837554-5-6
  1. Foreclosure—United States

  2. Mortgage Loans—United States

I. Alderman, Kimberly L., 1979- II. Title

Printed in the United States of America.

Preface

I first drafted these materials in preparation for a presentation I gave for the National Business Institute's Foreclosure, Short Sale and Loan Modification Compliance Update 2014. The information herein was intended to provide an overview of foreclosure litigation with a particular focus on defense strategies.

In this book, I begin by explaining the process of judicial foreclosure. The bulk of the publication is then devoted to defenses raised in foreclosure litigation. I include a final section on recent and pending appeals with the aim of providing a broad perspective on moving trends in the ever-evolving field of foreclosure defense.

Although I'm licensed in other jurisdictions, I've practiced foreclosure law in Wisconsin only. Because foreclosure law is specific to each state, it is not possible to give a comprehensive explanation of practice for every state in one reading. Rather, this publication discusses foreclosure defense generally, and is most useful to those residing or practicing in judicial foreclosure states. However, many of the defenses are common to both judicial and non-judicial foreclosure, but the means by which to raise them would be different in non-judicial foreclosure states.

Foreclosure Defenses was drafted in such a manner that its intended audience is both attorneys and non-attorneys (typically, borrowers). My purpose was to provide a survey of foreclosure litigation in judicial foreclosure states, and the practice of foreclosure defense therein. My aim was to make this information accessible to non-attorneys as well as to attorneys who are newer to foreclosure law and looking for a primer, perhaps to support an existing practice area such as bankruptcy or real estate transactions.

For the borrower reader, I beg your patience. I've attempted to present this work's ideas in as straightforward a manner as possible, but there are legal concepts that may be difficult to understand at first. No book can substitute for legal education and experience, and no pro se litigant stands as good of a chance as does one represented by able counsel. That does not, however, mean that a borrower should not take it upon himself to learn what he can about foreclosure law, if nothing else to know what to look for in his own case that might ultimately lead to a successful defense to foreclosure.

Even though a lawyer wrote this publication, and even if you are not a lawyer, I am not your lawyer. Nothing in this book is meant to substitute for an evaluation of your specific case by an able, state-licensed attorney. In other words, this book is legal knowledge, not legal advice.

Finally, this is a work in progress, which is why I first chose to publish it in the electronic format. If you come across something that you suspect is misleading, incorrect, or incomplete, please do contact me by email at kimberly@aldermanlawfirm.com to alert me of the suspected deficiency. This communication would be a great compliment, as it would let me know that someone is out there, reading. And, hopefully, finding the publication to be of some use.

Thank you for trusting me with your time and attention.

Table of Contents

Appendices

Part One:
The Judicial Foreclosure Process

State law determines the process for conducting mortgage foreclosures and, as a result, that process varies greatly from state to state. Wisconsin and a large number of other states follow a judicial foreclosure process, which is carried out through formal state court proceedings and can last anywhere from a few months to over a year.

Generally, a state that follows a judicial foreclosure process also follows the lien theory of mortgages. This means that the borrower owns legal and equitable title to the property and the lender holds a secured lien on the property through the mortgage. Compare how, in a non-judicial foreclosure, the foreclosure process may be largely or entirely carried out privately by the parties. Generally, in non-judicial foreclosure states, legal title to real estate remains with the mortgagee until the mortgage is fully paid.

After the borrower is significantly past due on his mortgage (usually 90 days, but this is within the discretion of the lender), the lender mails the borrower a notice of default (also called a notice of right to cure, or a notice of right to cure default, or even a demand letter). This document notifies the borrower that he breached the terms of the mortgage and the property will be subject to a foreclosure action. The letter further gives the borrower a certain number of days to cure the default, with the minimum time frame as determined by statute, and this varies significantly. Wisconsin law requires a 15-day right to cure period while Massachusetts, in some circumstances, requires that the borrower be allowed 150 days to cure. Either state law or the terms of the loan determines the relationship between the right to cure and when a foreclosure action can be initiated.

The plaintiff lender or servicer initiates the judicial foreclosure process by filing a summons and complaint in the court for the county where the property is located. A foreclosure summons provides notice to the defendant that an action for foreclosure has been initiated against him, and it proscribes the amount of time that he has to file his answer to the complaint. The complaint explains to the court why the plaintiff is entitled to a judgment of foreclosure on the property.

In a foreclosure action, the complaint names as defendants all the parties who have an interest in the property that the plaintiff wants the court to extinguish. This includes the borrower, the borrower's spouse, other private lien holders, tax lien holders, and tenants. A plaintiff may name senior lien holders[1] and guarantors (co-signers) of the loan, but this is not required. The decision of whether to do this will be influenced by whether the plaintiff is seeking a deficiency and/or money judgment.

Foreclosure complaints allege that the borrowers executed a note that the plaintiff now owns or has the right to enforce, that the note is secured by a mortgage on the subject property, that the borrowers have defaulted on the loan, and usually that the plaintiff has a superior claim to the defendants. The complaint also specifies whether the plaintiff is seeking a deficiency judgment, which is a money judgment for any debt not satisfied by the proceeds of the mortgage foreclosure sale. In some jurisdictions, such as some Wisconsin counties, the plaintiff must include a notice of mediation and mediation request form with the complaint, so that the defendant is notified of and able to request an optional mediation of the foreclosure action.

---

[1] A senior lien holder is a party that holds a superior interest in the property to the interests of other lien holders. For example, a primary mortgage note is senior to a second mortgage note or home equity loan.

The plaintiff must serve the summons and complaint on each defendant. The most common forms of valid service include personal service, service on a family member or other adult at the defendant's usual place of abode, and publishing a notice in a local newspaper or other accepted publication. The exact requirements for valid service vary from state to state, but usually service is affected via a process server or the county sheriff's office.

Once the defendant receives notice of the lawsuit against him, he has the fixed amount of time proscribed in the summons, but usually less than 30 days, to file an answer or a pre-answer motion, such as a motion to dismiss. The defendant may, however, move the court for an extension to file the answer beyond the standard timeline.

The answer is a legal document filed by a defendant who wishes to contest the allegations of the complaint. In the answer, a defendant responds to all the allegations of the complaint and explains his affirmative defenses. Each defendant answers individually, although when a husband and wife or relatives are both named, they often answer together. Quite often, junior lienholders do not answer at all, and simply wait out the foreclosure process.

In lieu of an answer, a defendant may file a motion to dismiss. The most popular basis for a motion to dismiss in foreclosure actions is a challenge to whether the plaintiff has standing. Another option is an allegation that the complaint is defective – that the plaintiff has failed to plead all the necessary elements of a foreclosure action. A motion to dismiss may also be premised on jurisdictional challenges. These defenses and others are further explored in the defenses section of these materials.

After filing the complaint, a foreclosure plaintiff must record a lis pendens with the recorder of deeds in the county where the property is located and the action is underway. A lis pendens is a public notice that a plaintiff has filed a lawsuit that concerns the title to real estate or those who hold an interest in that real estate. The purpose of this requirement is to make sure potential buyers of the real estate are aware of the legal challenges to the title of property and that holders of unrecorded encumbrances or interest in the real estate are notified of the lawsuit.

Failing to file a lis pendens may stall the foreclosure process. For example, a Wisconsin court cannot issue a judgment of foreclosure until 20 days after the plaintiff files the lis pendens. Wis. Stat. § 846.01. While state laws vary, the plaintiff's failure to file a lis pendens may make it vulnerable to a motion to dismiss from the defendant.

If a properly served defendant does not file an answer or otherwise resolve the foreclosure action, he will most likely be considered to be in default. In some jurisdictions this occurs automatically, but in others the plaintiff must request the clerk find the defendant in default. The plaintiff may then move the court for a default judgment. Typically, a court hearing is held to consider the motion. The resulting default judgment typically allows the plaintiff to obtain a judgment without having to prove his case, although a plaintiff typically has to demonstrate any money damages sought. There are still, usually, requirements that the plaintiff put the elements of its authority to foreclose on record, although the level of scrutiny that these submissions are exposed to tends to be low.

If a defendant does file an answer, the plaintiff is likely to file a motion for summary judgment (also called a motion for judgment on the pleadings). The defendant may defend by filing an opposition to that motion, and the plaintiff may typically respond to the opposition with a reply. The time frame for these filings varies by state. The court grants the motion for summary judgment if it holds that there is no dispute of material fact between the parties and judgment is appropriate as a matter of law. Much of the litigation regarding standing and other defenses to foreclosure occurs at the summary judgment phase because attorneys are often hired later in the judicial process, after the opportunity to file a motion to dismiss has passed. Further, borrowers may be motivated to drag on the foreclosure process, so their attorneys may elect a more passive approach in foreclosure litigation, responding only when so required.

While the foreclosure action is pending, the borrower generally retains the equitable right of redemption. This allows the borrower to pay the full mortgage debt plus costs at any time before the foreclosure sale. This payment may be in cash from the borrower, or from another bank via a refinance. The result of payment is an end to the foreclosure lawsuit. In Wisconsin, this right extends up to confirmation of the sale hearing, when the title is transferred to the new buyer (typically, the plaintiff lender). *Security State Bank v. Sechen*, et al., 288 Wis.2d 168, 707 N.W.2d 576 (2005).

Specific state statutes may create additional cure periods up until the time of foreclosure. For example, in Wisconsin, the borrower in an installment mortgage contract may resolve the foreclosure lawsuit and bring the loan current by paying the principle and interest due, with the costs. The period allowing for reinstatement of the loan may also be covered by common law or the terms of the mortgage. Generally, the borrower must pay past due principle and interest payments, penalty fees as specified under the terms of the loan, court costs, and attorney fees to bring the loan current. Reinstating the loan stops the foreclosure process.

To be clear, redemption means saving the property by paying off the lender, while curing is paying off the amount causing the default and saving the property by reinstating the loan.

In states with mediation programs, the borrower defendant may request mediation of the foreclosure dispute. Local rules determine whether participation in the program is mandatory or, as in Wisconsin, voluntary. Even if unsuccessful, mediation extends the timeframe for the foreclosure process because the court typically stops moving the case forward. For instance, a motion for summary judgment may remain undefended and pending for the months that it takes for the case to get through mediation. Or the court might issue a formal stay.

Ultimately, if the court determines that the plaintiff has established that the borrower is in default and the plaintiff has standing to foreclose, the court will grant a judgment of foreclosure. The contents of a judgment of foreclosure vary from state to state. In Wisconsin, the judgment includes a legal description of the property, a determination that the defendant defaulted on the mortgage, the amount the defendant owes to the plaintiff, the length of the period of statutory redemption, whether the plaintiff is entitled to a deficiency judgment, whether the property is a homestead, a determination that all other interest in the property is subordinate to the interest of the plaintiff, authorization for a sheriff sale, and an order that no party shall commit waste.

Although a borrower's right to cure will vary depending on the state the mortgage originated in as well as the terms of the loan, the right to cure generally does not extend to after the court issues a judgment of foreclosure. In some states, although the borrower is no longer legally entitled to simply bring the loan current and stop the foreclosure (although banks will often permit this), he may still pay off the entire balance of the loan, plus costs. This is called redemption, and the total amount required to redeem a property may be specified in the judgment of foreclosure.

The redemption period – the period during which a borrower defendant may still redeem his property by paying off the judgment amount – begins after the judgment for foreclosure is entered. The length of this period is governed by state statute and should be specified in the judgment of foreclosure. All states provide redemption periods before a foreclosure sale is held. A handful of states also provide a redemption period after the foreclosure sale has been completed. The factors that influence the length of the redemption period vary, but typically include the type of property (residential or commercial or abandoned or owner-occupied), whether the plaintiff is seeking a deficiency judgment, and whether the borrower waived the statutory redemption period in the loan agreement. Abbreviated redemption periods may be offered, such as in the case of foreclosures on land contracts, where Wisconsin offers a minimum redemption period of a mere 7 days.

It is uncommon for a borrower to come up with the cash necessary to redeem if he was unable to cure the default just months earlier. Other options for thwarting the foreclosure include selling the property and refinancing to pay off the judgment.

Once the redemption period expires, the mortgaged property is sold to satisfy the borrower's debts to the lender under the note. Often, this occurs by the court ordering the county sheriff to conduct a sheriff's sale. Whatever the mechanism for initiating the sale of the property, it cannot occur until after the statutory redemption period has passed. The plaintiff must further publish notice of the sale in accordance with state statute, and the sale is held open to the public. If there is a federal tax lien, the plaintiff must give 25 days notice to the IRS in order to ensure the interest will be extinguished.

Peculiarities of the foreclosure sale process will be governed by jurisdiction. In Wisconsin, foreclosed property that qualifies as exempt homestead[2] is sold after portions of the property not included in the homestead. Wis. Stat. § 846.11. If the sale of the non-exempt portion of the land satisfies the borrowers debts under the foreclosure judgment, then the borrower will be able to keep the homestead property.

---

[2] In Wisconsin, a homestead is defined as the dwelling and the land around it reasonably necessary to make use of the dwelling. Wis. Stat.§ 706.01(7).

At the foreclosure sale, the plaintiff usually provides the opening bid. This bid is often the amount of the judgment, which may exceed the value of the home. This is because the judgment amount usually includes late fees, escrow costs, plaintiff's attorney fees, and other costs of the proceedings. These additional costs, plus the accruing interest for the period in which payments have not been made, often results in a high balance. The plaintiff may be the only bidder at the foreclosure sale, or others may bid as well. As one would expect, the property goes to the highest bidder at the foreclosure sale. The buyer is usually required to post a deposit on the spot.

The foreclosure sale is not final and legally operative until the court confirms it, which the plaintiff must next request the court do. If the court determines that the property sold for fair value and that procedure was followed as to notice and other requirements, then it will confirm the sale. If there is a challenge at this stage, it is typically on the basis that the property did not sell for a fair value. In some jurisdictions, there is a presumption that the property sold for fair value if the lender waives any deficiency. Note that fair value at a foreclosure sale is not the same as fair market value, as some courts will confirm foreclosure sales for a price that is a mere 50% of the market value, especially if there were bidders other than the bank at the sale. If the court does not confirm the sale, the court will likely void it and order another. However, the court may confirm the sale even if the property sold for less than fair value so long as fair value is credited against the foreclosure judgment.

Once the sale is confirmed, the court calculates the amount of the deficiency the defendant owes the plaintiff, unless the plaintiff has waived deficiency or the property sold for a high enough price such that there is no deficiency. The deed to the property will be transferred to the new owner after the confirmation hearing, and the new owner will generally record the change in title. The rights of junior lien holders will be extinguished via the foreclosure process but, generally, the new owner will have purchased the property subject to the interest of any senior lien holder.

In the order of confirmation, the court typically orders the defendant to vacate the premises of the foreclosed property by a specified date. The timeframe for vacating the premises varies based on state law. Owner occupants are given significantly less time (as few as 5 days) than are tenant occupants (as many as 90 days). If the resident has not vacated the property by the court-ordered date, the purchaser may seek a writ of assistance to evict the resident from the foreclosed property. After the court issues the writ of assistance, the sheriff's office will generally remove the borrower from the premises of the foreclosed property via an eviction. The process of removing an uncooperative resident usually takes several months.

Part Two:
Defenses to Foreclosure

Chapter 1:
Lack of Standing

Black's Law Dictionary defines "standing" as a "party's right to make a legal claim or seek judicial enforcement of a duty or right." Standing represents the idea that not everyone concerned about a legal matter has a right to go to court and seek a remedy. Standing, colloquially, is a plaintiff's right to complain and get results in court.

Wisconsin's general rule on standing requires that the plaintiff be injured in fact and that the interest allegedly injured be arguably within the zone of interest to be protected or regulated by the statute or constitutional guarantee in question. *Moedern v. McGinnis*, 70 Wis. 2d 1056, 1067, 236 N.W.2d 240 (1975). The U.S. Supreme Court outlined standing rules broadly as requiring injury, causation, and redressability. *Lujan v. Defenders of Wildlife*, 504 U.S. 555 (1992).

Foreclosure actions for mortgage loans have two special requirements pertaining to standing: (1) the plaintiff must have the right to enforce the promissory note, and (2) the plaintiff must have a property interest in the real estate (i.e., via the mortgage).

The question of standing is appropriately raised in federal court via a Fed. R. Civ. P. 12(b)(1) motion to dismiss. Standing issues in federal courts implicate constitutional subject-matter jurisdiction because federal courts may only address cases or controversies under Article III of the constitution. *Common Cause of PA v. Pennsylvania*, 558 F.3d 249, 257 (3d Cir. 2009). In Wisconsin and other state courts, a motion to dismiss for plaintiff's failure to state a claim upon which relief may be granted is generally the most appropriate avenue for raising standing issues.

In theory, the only entity entitled to bring the foreclosure action is the holder of the mortgage. Because mortgages are usually bought and sold by several investors, identifying the last note holder in the chain can be difficult. A plaintiff seeking to foreclose whose name is not on the note and who cannot prove assignment will likely need to grapple with a standing defense, sometimes referred to as a "show me the note" defense.

State civil procedure rules may also require the Plaintiff to attach "all necessary documents" to the complaint. If the plaintiff does not attach the note and records of assignment, it may be impossible for the borrower to determine if the plaintiff is a proper party. The note and records of assignment are necessary documents to evaluate whether the case is complete and ripe for proceeding. In these instances, a motion to dismiss for failure to satisfy conditions precedent is an option to the failure to state a claim.

Standing requires an understanding of who the interested parties are and what comprises their interest. Thus, to grasp how the standing defense operates, a quick refresher on the players and instruments that dominate the mortgage industry is appropriate. Traditional secured lending involved a lender, borrower, a loan of money, a promissory note to evidence the loan, and collateral to minimize the lender's losses in the event of the borrower's default. If the lender wanted to transfer the contractual right to receive payment for the loan, then the note and collateral (in the form of a deed of trust or security deed) were transferred to a publicly identified buyer.

That system is now an anachronism. Today, the secondary market for mortgages is populated with mortgage-backed securities, collateralized debt obligations, and real estate mortgage investment conduits. Their purveyors are nominees or servicers. In many cases, the defendant homeowner may not even recognize the entity seeking foreclosure.

Mortgage-backed securities or MBS are instruments that arose following the great depression. MBS are produced through the process of securitization. Securitization describes the pooling of contractual debt, bundling the debt into different categories of risk, and then selling the bundles to investors. Mortgage-backed securities may include interests in more than 1,000 mortgages. Securitization allows investors to choose the level of risk they would like to take on and provides mortgage-holders (usually banks) access to funds.

The process of securitization separates the original borrower (homeowner) from the original lender (bank). It creates indirect ownership of mortgage loans through ownership of bundles of mortgage loans. The Federal Housing Authority (FHA) and Government-Sponsored Enterprises like Freddie Mac and Fannie Mae insure these pools of residential loans. The process of securitization may involve loan splitting. Loan splitting is the separation of the promissory note (interest in debt) from the mortgage deed or mortgage lien (interest in property).

A collateralized debt obligation (CDO) is a form of securitization. Again, debts are amassed, bundled, and sold to investors. Collateralized debt obligations are unique in that they bundle different types of debt together including mortgages, auto loans, and corporate bonds, among others. Income from the debt bundle is then distributed to investors in a defined sequence.

Another financial tool, Real Estate Mortgage Investment Conduits (or REMICs) was born in the mid-1980s. REMICs are trusts that pool mortgage loans and enjoy pass-through taxation. Pass through taxation means that the income is only taxed at the level of the individual investors and is not also subject to corporate taxation. REMICs, like mortgage-backed securities, obscure the ownership interest in the mortgage. The "owner" of the loan that forms part of a MBS or REMIC-qualified trust is typically a trustee for the beneficiaries who are certificate owners or investors.

In the 80s and 90s, investment banks successfully petitioned the government to allow subprime mortgages to be bundled and sold as mortgage-backed securities. Subprime loans are essentially high-risk loans where the borrowers are more likely to default or the loans have poor quality collateral. By 2006, the significant majority of subprime loans were mortgage-backed securities. From 2000 to 2006, government programs encouraging lending coupled with neglect in enforcement of consumer protections resulted in the subprime market tripling its share of the overall mortgage market.

So, what does all this mean? The securitization of mortgages has resulted in the overwhelming use of servicers, for one thing. The servicer is an entity under contract with the owner of the loan to collect payments, ensure taxes and insurance are paid, and perform other tasks related to administration of a mortgage. Sometimes, depending on the terms of the contract between the lender and the servicer, the servicer is tasked with protecting the collateral and declaring a default and foreclosing/liquidating the collateral when appropriate. The terms of the contract between the servicer and owner vary and are private, so the borrower (and the borrower's attorney) are now sometimes necessarily unclear on what party has authority to foreclose on a note. The authority of the servicer to bring a foreclosure action has received disparate treatment in different states.

Another issue arising out of the securitization of mortgages is MERS. In 1993, Mortgage Electronic Registration Service, Inc. (MERS) was established in order to eliminate the need for preparation and recording of traditional mortgage sales with the register of deeds – essentially a response to the frequent and bulk trading of mortgages. MERS acts as "nominee" for the original lender and "mortgagee" of the mortgagor-borrower. It remains a static owner of record of the security deed or deed of trust no matter how many times the mortgage of the loan servicing rights are transferred. The transfers of rights in the collateral securing a mortgage loan within MERS are not quality-controlled or publicly scrutinized – it's all internal and private, unlike the traditional system where paper assignments were publicly recorded. Some attorneys who have performed thorough discovery on MERS foreclosures have reported that a lack of quality control is reflected in the information provided to the borrower and court.

The important thing to take away from this system of nominees, servicers, trusts, securities, REMICs and mortgage-backed securities is that the plaintiff seeking to foreclose may not be the true owner, and the true owner may have trouble proving its ownership. A lack of publicly accessible documentation to determine who has the authority to foreclose may leave real interests in property vague. To show injury in fact and access to an enforceable legal remedy, the party attempting to foreclose should be the mortgage holder. The mortgage holder owns and holds the note at the time foreclosure proceedings commence and has the right to enforce the note. However, in modern practice the focus is on the note – because the mortgages follow it. The reasoning is that a mortgage without a note is useless.

The plaintiff has the burden to prove its standing. *James Talcott, Inc. v. Allahabad Bank, Ltd.,* 444 F.2d 451, 457 (5th Cir. 1971). The first requirement for standing in a foreclosure case is the contractual right to enforce the promissory note. If a note is endorsed with an identified payee, only the entity identified in the mortgage documents and in possession of the note has the right to enforce it. UCC § 3-205(a). If a note is "endorsed in blank," then it is payable to the bearer of the note, and only the previous owner needs to be named on the note as transferring its interest to the bearer, who is not named. UCC § 3-205(b).

Each of these methods of assignment assumes that the mortgage documents are available. However, in practice, floods, fires, and the absentmindness of lenders may lead to the documents being lost or unavailable. UCC § 3-309 deals with lost instruments. It permits enforcement of an instrument that is not possessed if (1) the person seeking to enforce the instrument was entitled to enforce it prior to the loss of possession or acquired ownership from a person who was entitled to enforce prior to the loss, (2) the loss was not due to a transfer or lawful seizure, and (3) the person cannot reasonably obtain the instrument because it was destroyed, cannot be found, or in the wrongful possession of another person who cannot be served process.

The plaintiff must prove more than the assignment to prevail. He or she must also prove the terms of the instrument and the person's right to enforce its terms. UCC § 3-308 which governs signature verification applies to the case as if the person seeking enforcement had produced the instrument. The UCC also mandates that the person required to pay the instrument be adequately protected against loss due to a subsequent third party claim. Adequate protection may be provided by any reasonable means.

The lack of signature on the instrument can also impede standing. The recipient transferee of an unendorsed instrument must prove chain of possession. Simply put, this is because the transferee's rights derive from the transferor's rights. UCC § 3-308 only presumes payment is owed when a holder produces the instrument, and a transferee is not a holder. In other words, if the terms of the instrument do not identify that payment is owed to a particular person and the transferee simply possesses the note, chain of possession should usually be established before the note can be enforced.

Agents who are not owners or holders have the burden to show specific authority to initiate a foreclosure on behalf of the owner. Alternatively, an agent may show the note is assigned to it for purposes of collection. Given this, foreclosure agents and servicers do not automatically have standing but must demonstrate authority to act for the owner. See e.g., *In re Jacobson*, 402 B.R. 359 (Bankr. W.D. Wash. 2009).

This issue came to the fore in *Mortgage Electronic Registration Systems, Inc. v. Lisa Marie Chong*, et al., Case No. 2:09-CV-00661-KJD-LRL (Dist. Ct. Nev. 2009). The District Court of Nevada found, "Since MERS provided no evidence that it was the agent or nominee for the current owner of the beneficial interest in the note, it has failed to meet its burden of establishing that it is a real party in interest with standing."

There is no clear consensus on the extent to which agency to foreclose can be conferred to a servicer. Investors and servicers contend this may be accomplished through their pooling and servicing agreements (PSAs). These are the service agreements that arrange a servicer to collect payments from borrowers and distribute income to investors.

One view is that authority to foreclose cannot be based only on a services agreement. See *U.S. Bank v. Ibanez*, 458 Mass. 637, 649, 941 N.E.2d 40, 52 (Mass. App. 2011). In Ibanez, US Bank, as trustee, foreclosed on Ibanez before receiving formal assignment of mortgage. US Bank claimed that the PSA established its authority to foreclose. The Court held that even though "the underlying promissory notes serve as financial instruments generating a potential income stream for investors, ... the mortgages securing these notes are still legal title to someone's home or farm and must be treated as such."

In contrast, certain courts have focused on the mechanism in the PSA that gives the servicer the right to assignment once a loan goes into default. In these arrangements, the default is a trigger that assigns the note to the servicer. At that point, the servicer becomes a real party in interest. In *Green Tree Servicing LLC v. Sanders*, the Court explained, "for the purpose of enforcing the loan obligation, [the servicer] became the holder and owner of the note and mortgage." No. 2005-CA-000371-MR, 2006 WL 2033668 (Ky. App. July 21, 2006) (unpublished case, cited to in *Bruner v. Discover Bank*, 360 S.W.3d 774, 777 (Ky. App., 2012)).

It is good practice to check the assignment rules for servicers in the state where the property resides if the plaintiff is a trustee for mortgage-backed securities. The complaint may look like: "X Bank as Trustee for Y Asset-Backed Bond Series 2006-V" and this should initiate deeper digging into the assignment and transfer history.

The second requirement for standing in a foreclosure case is property interest in real estate. This property interest usually comes from the mortgage.

When notes are split from the collateral property that is intended to insure them, determining property interest in real estate can be onerous. That is because most jurisdictions presume the note holder is the holder of the collateral property interest. It is commonly said that the Note "wags the tail", or brings the interest in the property along with it. Remember, the mortgage follows the note, and not the other way around. Interestingly, the "mort" in "mortgage" comes from the Latin word for death (e.g. "mortal" and "mortician") because the mortgage deed dies with repayment of the note. Despite the seemingly essential link between the two, securitization has made splitting of the note and mortgage a practical reality.

Mergers can also blur who the party entitled to enforce the note is. Proof of the merger is required to show the new entity is the note holder. In the event of merger, the identity of the new entity is considered one with the original lender. This is another product of the mortgage securitization industry and the rapid growth of subprime mortgages. As corporations rose and fell, their interests were transferred subject to not only assignments but also mergers and trusts and other means that complicate identifying all parties with an interest in the note.

This is important because if more than one party has an interest in the note, they must all be party to the foreclosure action. In the case of successful prosecution, the foreclosure cannot extinguish the rights of a party not named as a defendant to the action. Further, just because a defendant is subject to suit by the first party with interest in a note, this doesn't preclude the second party from coming back later and attempting to enforce the note separately.

MERS created an environment that is rife for problems like the ones described – it can become almost impossible to determine who the interest holder(s) is(are) in a note, to the exclusion of others. This was especially true when it was MERS foreclosing on the notes. The problem of MERS pursuing foreclosures grew to such proportions that MERS ultimately struck a deal with the U.S. Treasury to desist in its pursuit of foreclosure actions on behalf of mortgage holders. The deal effectively nullified the debate over standing with MERS. Still, understanding how MERS incited numerous cases involving standing questions is essential to competent reading of prior case law. Its discussion here is not intended as model for future litigation, but rather as a means for discussing the sometimes-complicated issues that arise in challenging standing to pursue foreclosure. The controversy over lenders' use of the MERS system is a case study in foreclosure defense based on standing.

MERS is not a lender. It is a computer system for electronically registering mortgages in a private database. This registry monitors approximately 60 million homes nationwide, about half the nation's homes. MERS acts as a market, permitting mortgage holders to easily sell and trade mortgage-backed securities. Although the MERS system does not own the mortgages it registers and exchanges, members using MERS agree that MERS acts as a "nominee" for the owner of the mortgage at any given time while the mortgage remains in the MERS system. A nominee is an entity that represents the interests of another in a limited way.

MERS heralded many changes in the financial industry. Previously, exchanges of liens against a property were accomplished by filing the change of ownership with the register of deeds and paying a fee. These exchanges were public and could be checked easily by making a request or visit to the register of deeds. In contrast, MERS allowed mortgages to change hands quickly and privately, without public scrutiny.

MERS members treated it as the presumed "holder" of the promissory note – despite not being the true owner. MERS nomination was created to transfer assignment of mortgage and promissory note to an investment trust without the formality of actually endorsing the promissory notes and properly assigning the mortgages to the investment trusts. Stunningly, some companies made it their practice to destroy the promissory note once it entered the MERS system.

When MERS began assigning servicers the mortgage documents to foreclose, defense attorneys argued that MERS could only assign the interest it had in the mortgage – its status as nominee. See *Federal National Mortgage Ass'n v. Bradbury*, 32 A.3d 1014, 2011 ME 120 (2011); *GMAC Mortgage LLC v. Neu* No. 50-2008-CA-040805XXXX-MB (Fla. Circ. Ct. Dec. 10, 2009) (cited nationally because of a deposition in which a loan servicer employee discussed robo-signing practices). In order to remedy this conundrum, some in the mortgage industry created documents that would make it appear as though the servicer was a real party in interest. The servicer would recreate (i.e. fabricate) the promissory note and then assign the deed of trust to the newly created note. Alternatively, plaintiff loan servicers would use copies of new promissory notes as originals or submit affidavits to the courts indicating the original note was lost. These practices, in a nutshell, are fraudulent.

There was difficulty creating the assignment from MERS to the loan servicer in many cases. This is particularly true when original lenders are in bankruptcy and cannot assign assets. Loan servicers responded by creating mortgage assignments that appeared to have come from MERS but were actually robo-signed in-house by the servicer. Robo-signers are people who sign large volumes of affidavits without personal knowledge about the facts in those affidavits (even though the affidavits purport that they do). Robo-signing was proof that some foreclosing entities did not have standing to foreclose. Again, this practice was tantamount to defrauding homeowners and the court in foreclosure proceedings.

In response to robo-signing malfeasance, the National Mortgage Settlement was negotiated between 49 states (all minus Oklahoma) and five national lenders (Ally/GMAC, Bank of America, Citi, JPMorgan Chase, and Wells Fargo). It exposed the shortcuts systematically taken by lenders during foreclosure proceedings. It is now well settled and apparent that MERS has no beneficial interest in the mortgage note or mortgage. Courts such as the Supreme Court of Arkansas have ruled that MERS cannot be the mortgagee on a deed filed in the property records because of this lack of beneficial interest. See *Mortg. Elec. Registration Sys., Inc. v. S.W. Homes of Ark.*, 2009 Ark. 152 (2009).

All this suggests that when the chain of ownership of a note is not well known, problems multiply. Defendants may challenge the allegation that securitization occurred at all. If the register of deeds has the original lender listed as the mortgage holder, the defense may claim no further assignment occurred. This puts the plaintiff in the position to prove its place in the chain of ownership, preferably occupying the final link. Defendants may also challenge whether the loan was actually assigned to the trust once it entered the securitization process. This can include a challenge to the proper form of the transfer.

Absent chain of ownership, hidden interests may also go unrecognized. For example, the loan may have been the subject of a credit default swap. A credit default swap (CDS) is a financial agreement where the seller of a CDS bond will compensate the buyer in the event of a loan default. The buyer of the CDS bond pays fees to the seller and receives a payout if the loan defaults. It would also be unclear whether any paydowns or payoffs of the note occurred as the result of insurance claims.

If a note has entered the MERS system, this is a red flag for standing issues. Fabricated promissory notes are almost always traceable back to the MERS system. Checking the status of a note in the MERS system is possible by obtaining the MIN, or mortgage identification number. The MERS system can be searched here: https://www.mers-servicerid.org/sis/. The registry should reflect the name of the investment trust ostensibly in control of the promissory note.

Next, if the note has been warehoused by MERS, the defendant should demand the plaintiff produce the original promissory note. Unfortunately, in some cases, the note will be mocked up to appear authentic. To test the authenticity of the note, compare the note's endorsements with the MIN record. Some notes falsely represent that multiple endorsements were made when the reality is that most promissory notes are never endorsed. They are endorsed in blank (endorsed without an identified payee) and transferred to an investment trust. If this discrepancy appears, the validity of the note should be investigated further.

Third, allonges are often used to display fabricated endorsements. An allonge is a separate document attached to the note used to keep record of multiple endorsements. Fabricators may make it appear that the original lender to the loan servicer endorsed the note. Allonges may be also be robo-signed by the loan servicer in favor of the loan servicer. The absence of dates or warranties of corporate authority are red flags.

Fourth, take a look at the assignments. Employees of the loan servicer and not MERS may have executed assignments. Self-assignment is an effort to place the servicer into the chain of title. Absent the original promissory note or assignment of the mortgage, the servicer does not have standing to foreclose. Self-assignments by the servicers may become apparent if the notary public's state of registration is not Virginia because Virginia where MERS is centrally located.

Fifth, request an accounting. Scrutinize the records for improper charges, force-placed insurance, and inappropriate property inspections. Look also for failure to credit payments under trial loan modifications.

Sixth, check online for class actions brought against creditors and their agents. Results may provide other defects to look for.

Given the complicated interplay of actors and loan mutations unknown to the borrower, the defense of standing should garner serious consideration when the plaintiff is any entity besides the original mortgage lender.

Chapter 2:
Failure to Join Indispensible Parties

An indispensable party is a party required in the foreclosure proceedings for the court to determine the complete rights and obligations of all parties. Courts consider several factors to determine whether a party is indispensable and these factors may be prescribed by statute or rule. See e.g., Wis. Stat. § 803.03(3)(a)-(d); Fed. R. Civ. P. 19.

Because mortgage notes may be transferred or assigned multiple times, multiple indispensable parties may exist. Importantly, the burden is on the plaintiff to show the chain of mortgage ownership. The complaint must demonstrate who is entitled to bring a foreclosure action and name all other interested parties as defendants. Even if the plaintiff has an exclusive interest in the mortgage note, he must demonstrate that he is the only party permitted to foreclose.

Filing a motion to dismiss the complaint for failure to join indispensable parties accomplishes three things for the defendant. First, by ensuring everyone with an interest has a voice in the foreclosure proceedings, the borrower defendant prevents another party from appearing later and seeking a judgment on the same mortgage loan. Second, forcing the plaintiff to identify and name all interested parties may delay the foreclosure. This provides additional time for the borrower to come up with necessary funds. Third, the chain of ownership may uncover the plaintiff's lack of ownership interest and, thus, standing to bring the claim. This is an unlikely result but occasionally a servicer will initiate foreclosure proceedings without having a real interest in the property.

In the Fifth Circuit case of *Eva Sudhoff v. Federal National Mortgage Association*, Mrs. Sudhoff signed off on the mortgage although she was not liable under the note. *Sudoff v. Federal National Mortgage Association*, No. 5D05-3137 (Fla. 5th DCA 2006). The foreclosure proceedings did not name her, and the Fifth Circuit held that they were therefore only effective in foreclosing on Mr. Sudhoff's interest in the home. It is an obvious test – were Mrs. Sudhoff's interests affected by the action? Yes, and she should therefore have been named on the action. Indispensible parties who are not named in a foreclosure action cannot have their rights affected by the action; they remain in the same position they were in prior to the foreclosure. This is why it is so important to explore and establish whether any other parties may have an arguable interest in the note, mortgage, or property.

Indispensable parties may include other mortgage holders, lien holders including tax liens asserted by the IRS or the state, spouses with marital property interests (especially important if divorce proceedings are pending), and tenants with leasehold interests. The latter is why you will see that many foreclosure actions name "Unknown Tenants," because the plaintiff does not know who is living in a home who may have his rights affected by the action.

If the complaint does not state how the mortgage note has been transferred or assigned, a motion to dismiss the complaint for failure to join indispensable parties is appropriate. In Wisconsin, the defendant may raise this defense in the answer or by motion. Wis. Stat. § § 802.06(2); 802.06(8)(b). The motion can request dismissal or, alternatively, a "more definite statement" from the plaintiff regarding parties in interest.

Chapter 3:
Failure to Follow Right to Cure Requirements

Generally, the source of right to cure requirements can be either a state statute or the terms of the mortgage. For example, Wisconsin state law requires that a lender give a borrower 15 days notice of his intent to file a foreclosure action. This creates a 15-day right to cure period for the borrower. It is not uncommon for mortgages to contain similar terms of notice requirements. As a result, a lender's failure to properly notify a borrower of a cure period could be a violation of state law, a breach of contract, or both.

If a plaintiff initiates a foreclosure action without complying with the right to cure requirements, a defendant can use the violation as an affirmative defense. This means that a borrower must plead this defense in his answer to the lender's foreclosure complaint. If the borrower does not affirmatively plead complaint. If the borrower does not affirmatively plead this defense, he might inadvertently waive the defense. However, state rules of civil procedure generally allow the defendant to timely amend his answer to include additional affirmative defenses.

If a defendant establishes the affirmative defense that the plaintiff violated statutory right to cure requirements, the court might dismiss the suit. In Wisconsin, for instance, a lender's failure to comply with the previously mentioned 15-day notice has resulted in dismissal of the case. See *Indianhead Motors v. Brooks*, 2006 WI App 266, 726 N.W.2d 352 (2006).

Courts may also dismiss a case for failure to follow the right to cure requirements in the terms of a mortgage. In *Kurian v. Wells Fargo Bank* (2013), a Florida appellate court reversed summary judgment of foreclosure because the defendant pled and sufficiently proved the affirmative defense that plaintiff failed to comply with the notice of default requirements in the terms of the mortgages.

Chapter 4:
Not in Default

The best defense to any foreclosure action is payment. If the borrower made the payments that the lender claims he or she has missed, the borrower can defend against the foreclosure action by simply proving that the payments were made. However unlikely it sounds that a borrower would have paid certain sums and the lender would still foreclose, it does happen. The borrower may not have paid everything, but it is possible that they have paid enough to make a foreclosure action premature under the terms of the note.

Additionally, the borrower may pay the amount of the default after the foreclosure action has commenced. The ability to bring a mortgage current, thereby avoiding foreclosure, is called the right to cure. State and federal law provides borrowers with a right to

State and federal law provides borrowers with a right to cure any default before the lender can foreclose. The length of this right to cure varies by state. In order to exercise the right to cure, the borrower must pay the entire defaulted amount, as well as any costs and fees. Before a judgment is entered reinstating the mortgage, all potential counterclaims should be raised in the answer. In the event of a subsequent default, res judicata may prevent raising the counterclaims in a second foreclosure action. See *Kowske v. Ameriquest Mortgage Company*, 319 Wis. 2d 500, 767 N.W. 409 (2009).

Further, lenders do not always (some foreclosure defense attorneys would argue usually) calculate the amount in default correctly. The borrower or his attorney should always confirm the figures provided by the lender as to the amount in default. There are many different fees that factor into the total default amount, and it is not uncommon for lenders to overcharge for authorized fees or charge unauthorized fees. Excessive and unauthorized fees may include escrow overcharges, incorrectly calculated interest fees, improperly applied late fees, or unauthorized "drive by" property inspections. Additionally, lenders may have added additional products or services to the mortgage that the borrower is unaware of, such as forced place insurance.

In these situations, the borrower's answer will deny allegations in the complaint regarding the amount in default and the lender's right to foreclose under the terms of the mortgage. Formally, the borrower will assert the defense of failure to state a claim upon which relief may be granted." The borrower will attach proof of payment and any information regarding inappropriate charges to the answer. It is worth noting that, in some jurisdictions, any motion to dismiss must be filed before filing an answer.

Assuming payment has been made, the lender will probably move for a voluntary dismissal. If not, the borrower may file a motion to dismiss (or for summary judgment in) the foreclosure action. In support of such a motion, defendant-borrowers produce copies of canceled checks, confirmation numbers from payments made over the phone, or confirmation statements from payments made online. If the borrower can prove that the lender accepted the allegedly missing payments, the lender will have no right to foreclose and the case should be dismissed.

Chapter 5:
Waiver and Estoppel

Estoppel prevents a lender from misleading a borrower to the borrower's detriment. It is an equitable defense concerned with preventing injustice to the borrower. In Wisconsin, circuit courts have discretion to exercise equitable powers to prevent injustice in foreclosure proceedings. *Harvest State Bank v. ROI Investments*, 228 Wis. 733, 598 N.W.2d 571 (1999).

The typical elements of estoppel are: (1) a statement or promise is made which; (2) is reasonably expected to induce action or forbearance of a definite and substantial character from the borrower; (3) the borrower justifiably relies on the statement or promise and (4) as a result of the reliance the borrower suffers a substantial detriment.

One situation where this defense arises involves an agreement not to foreclose. In such cases, the lender agrees to accept a lower monthly payment from the borrower, promises not to foreclose if those payments are made, and then forecloses anyway in spite of the borrower's compliance with the new terms. See e.g., *Mutual Federal S. & L. v. American Med. Services*, 66 Wis. 2d 210, 223 N.W.2d 921 (1974). Allowing the lender to renege on the bargain it proposed would be unjust, and so, estoppel is presented as a defense in these instances.

The example above may also be characterized as a waiver, or an intentional relinquishment of rights by the lender. The difference is that a waiver can be made implicitly, whereas estoppel usually requires an affirmative promise. If a borrower starts paying less than the full payment owed, or on the 15th of the month rather than the first, and the lender allows this pattern to continue for some time, an argument can be made that the lender waived its right to the initial repayment terms.

Waiver may be express or implied and is treated as a modification to the existing contract. Implied waiver requires a reasonable inference that the lender has voluntarily given up certain rights. Note, however, that most lenders now include a non-waiver provision in the mortgage agreement explicitly stating that failure to respond to a default cannot be deemed a waiver.

The policy reason for these defenses is simply to prevent powerful lenders from taking advantage of unsophisticated borrowers who reasonably rely on their lender for information.

Chapter 6:
Laches

Laches is a common law defense that prevents plaintiffs from waiting an unreasonable length of time before filing the lawsuit. It is similar to a statute of limitations but independent of it. Either or both may be raised. A laches defense argues, simply, "The plaintiff waited too long, and it would be unfair to allow it to recover at this point."

There is no exact length of time that must pass before a defendant can use a laches defense. Rather, the defendant generally must show (1) that the plaintiff unreasonably delayed in filing the lawsuit and (2) that the defendant was determinately affected by the delay.

Laches is an affirmative defense, so the defendant generally must raise it in his answer or a pre-answer motion. In *Zizzo v. Lakeside Steel & Mfg. Co.* 2008 WI App 69, 752 N.W.2d 889 (2008), a Wisconsin appellate court determined that laches could be used as an affirmative defense in a mortgage foreclosure lawsuit; however, the appeal was ultimately decided on other grounds.

Chapter 7:
Predatory Lending

Predatory lending occurs when lenders engage in practices that are unfair, deceptive, or fraudulent. These practices, which typically arise during the loan origination process, target unsophisticated buyers. Any given loan is likely predatory if it charges an unreasonable interest rate and fees, contains abusive terms, fails to take the borrower's ability to repay into account, or illegally targets specific groups such as women or minorities. In essence, a predatory loan sets the borrower up to fail.

Predatory lending practices often begin well before any loan agreement is entered into. When initially soliciting clients, predatory lenders often aggressively solicit specific neighborhoods, including those with a high concentration of low income and minority individuals. Other schemes include engaging in door-to-door solicitation of home improvements for which the contractor arranges the financing then either fails to complete the work or does a sub-par job, or convincing borrowers to flip – or frequently refinance – their mortgages despite the flip not providing any economic benefit to the borrowers. Finally, predatory lenders may steer borrowers to high rate loans when there is a more affordable option.

The terms of a loan may also be an indication of predatory loan practices. Such terms may include the imposition of penalties for prepayment, unreasonably high interest rates, high fees and closing costs, padded costs, duplicative charges, and the financing of such fees and costs. In some cases, brokers will impose an inflated interest rate with the intent that the lender will pay the broker a kickback or "yield spread premium." Falsified loan applications and forged signatures on loan documents are also obvious giveaways of fraudulent and predatory lending.

Loans can also be predatory based on their operation. Typically, a predatory loan will provide no apparent benefit to the consumer. For example, some predatory loans use balloon payments to entice borrowers into an ultimately unaffordable refinance which forces eventual foreclosure. Other predatory lending tactics with no apparent benefit to the consumer include the shifting of unsecured debt into mortgage debt, and providing loans in excess of 100% loan-to-value.

The mechanics of a defense based on predatory lending will be dependent on the unique facts of predatory lending demonstrated in each situation. The defense of procedural unconscionability should be used where the contracting parties failed to have a true meeting of the minds when drafting the contract. This defense arises from the fact that, in order to be valid, every contract requires mutual assent. In some states, in order to effectively plead procedural unconscionability, a party must also show substantive unconscionability. Substantive unconscionability pertains to the reasonableness of the contract terms themselves (as opposed to the negotiating disadvantage or something outside the contract).

State consumer fraud acts may also be applicable to predatory lending. If a predatory loan violates a state consumer fraud act, the resulting mortgage may be deemed invalid. See, e.g. The New Jersey Consumer Fraud Act (CFA); *Associates Home Equity Services v. Troup*, 343 N.J. Super. 254, 778 A.2d 529 (2001) (mortgage found to be invalid when it represented a mismatch between the needs and capacity of the borrower). State fraud acts are often violated by door-to-door solicitation of home improvement "contractors" such as those in Associates Home Equity Services. Obviously, the exact scope of state legislation will vary, and predatory loans may comprise the proscribed practices in some acts but not others. Further, the remedies will presumably vary. Additionally, note that there may be multiple applicable acts. In Wisconsin there are the Unfair and Deceptive Acts and Practices Act as well as the Wisconsin Consumer Act.

A defense based on predatory lending practices may also be asserted under common law concepts such as fraud, duress, undue influence, misrepresentation, or negligent supervision of employees. For example, a borrower may allege that the mortgage broker was acting as agent for lender or servicer and lied about the terms of the Note/Mortgage, thereby tricking the borrower into signing them. Negligent supervision of employees has been tacked on when a reasonable person could have foreseen the type of injuries that occurred. Proof of these common law concepts in the context of a mortgage or note may invalidate the contract.

Finally, usury – loans that are unethical or immoral, often due to exorbitant interest rates – is a defense in equity. If a borrower can show that the rate of interest he or she is paying on the loan is unethically high or higher than the rate allowed for by law, the Court may find it to be usurious and dismiss the action. Usury laws vary state by state. Some states have eliminated usury laws altogether, but still maintain laws governing the maximum interest that may be charged for various loans. A successful claim for usury may also implicate claims under RICO, which prohibits racketeering. Racketeering includes usurious credit transactions. However, RICO is a federal criminal law, and violation is not a per se defense to foreclosure.

Chapter 8:
Breach of Duty of Good Faith and Fair Dealing

Mortgage contracts impart extensive power and discretion to the lender. The duty of good faith and fair dealing is the golden rule of contract law – it requires that neither party infringe on the other party's rights to receive benefits under the contract. The touchstones of good faith are honesty and reasonableness.

An equitable defense, the breach of a duty of good faith can take several forms. Generally, behaviors demonstrating a breach include: evasion of the spirit of the bargain, lack of diligence and slacking off, willful rendering of imperfect performance, abuse of a power to specify terms, and interference with or failure to cooperate in the other party's performance. *Wisconsin*

Housing and Economic Development Authority v. Tri-Corp., 332 Wis.2d 804 (2011).

A contracting party can breach its duty of good faith even if it does not violate any express term of the contract. *Foseid v. State Bank of Cross Plains*, 197 Wis.2d 772, 796, 541 N.W.2d 203 (Ct. App. 1995). It acts as a general prohibition against the creativity of malicious people in seeking to circumvent agreements. Whereas other breaches rely on the terms of the contract itself, the duty of good faith goes further and governs conduct not covered within the four corners of the contract. Bear in mind, however, that a party cannot complain that acts specifically contemplated by the contract constitute bad-faith conduct. For example, a lender's refusal to consider alternatives to foreclosure is not considered bad faith if the contract does not require it and the lender has made no representations to the contrary.

Chapter 9:
Breach of Fiduciary Duty

A fiduciary relationship requires that one party act for another's benefit. The duties of a fiduciary include loyalty and reasonable care. Common fiduciary relationships include attorney and client, trust and trustee, and guardian and ward. Reasonable care usually pertains to appropriately holding assets within the fiduciary's control. In the foreclosure context, the borrower may assert the lender was a fiduciary and breached its duty to act in the borrower's best interests.

Importantly, the mere existence of a borrower-lender contract and borrower-lender relationship does not necessarily create a fiduciary duty. However, a fiduciary duty may be created by special contract terms or by a special relationship between the borrower and lender. *Production Credit Ass'n of Lancaster v.*

Croft, 143 Wis.2d 746, 752, 423 N.W.2d 544 (Ct. App.1988).

The elements of a claim for breach of fiduciary duty are: (1) the defendant owed the plaintiff a fiduciary duty; (2) the defendant breached that duty; and (3) the breach of duty caused the plaintiff's damage. *Berner Cheese Corp. v. Krug*, 312 Wis. 2d 251 (2008). The underlying interest is to provide unsophisticated parties in need of advice the assurance that an advisor will act in their best interests.

The circumstances that give rise to a fiduciary duty vary by state. In Wisconsin, a contract may establish a fiduciary relationship if it vests in the lender control of the borrower's property. This comes with an important caveat: restrictions on the borrower's operation do not establish a fiduciary relationship if they are reasonably necessary to protect the lender's interest in the collateral and are made in good faith. *PCA v. Croft*, 143 Wis.2d 746, 753-54, 423 N.W.2d 544 (Ct. App. 1988). For instance, the lender may hold the borrower's money in escrow to pay for taxes and insurance on the property, as this is reasonably necessary for the lender to protect its interest in the mortgage.

Chapter 10:
Statutes of Limitation

Statutes of limitation specify a time limit to seek relief via a lawsuit. If a plaintiff does not file within the applicable statute of limitations, and the court does not find a reason to "toll" the statute, the case will be dismissed. Each state has a different statute of limitations as to foreclosure actions. Often, the applicable statute of limitations is for contract or debt collection, which is commonly 6 years but varies.

Sometimes, however, states have statutes of limitations that are specific to foreclosure. For example, in Florida, a lender must file for foreclosure within 5 years of the time the borrower defaulted on the loan. Compare New Jersey, which allows lenders to file until the earliest of 6 years from the last set mortgage payment date, 20 years from default, or 36 years from the recording of the mortgage.

Depending on the court, the statute of limitations may or may not be considered jurisdictional. Also, the statute of limitations may or may not be an affirmative defense that must be raised in an answer or pre-answer motion, else it may be considered waived.

Chapter 11:
Strict Procedural Defenses

Florida has a requirement that an out-of-state plaintiff file a bond in order to maintain an action in the state. Fla. Stat. § 57.011. The defendant may raise a procedural objection in the answer that the plaintiff failed to file this bond. The plaintiff then has 20 days to pay the bond. The purpose of the bond requirement is to assure a prevailing borrower can recover costs from the plaintiff. The $100 bond enables a very nominal form of cost shifting if the defendant borrower succeeds on the merits. Borrowers' attorneys appreciate this defense because it is easy to raise and, if the plaintiff fails to respond, the suit may be dismissed.

Although the author is unaware of other states in which this particular defense is available, it is illustrative of the point that every state has specific procedural rules that must be followed in litigation, and that these procedural rules may serve as the basis for a defense in foreclosure.

Another strictly procedural defense that is worth noting pertains to unlicensed lenders. Some borrowers have defended on the grounds that the lender was not a licensed financial entity in their home state at the time the mortgage was issued. In *GMAC Mortgage, LLC, v. Clyde Fraser, et al.* Case No. 2:2010cv02430 (N.J. Dis. Ct. 2010), the Superior Court of New Jersey, Appellate Division, held that while unlicensed lenders may not enforce their debt instruments, licensed assignees of the instruments can.

Chapter 12:
Failure to Effect Good Services

Another mechanism that will stall but not prevent foreclosure is a motion to dismiss for failure to effect good service. If all parties to the foreclosure action were not validly served, a defendant may be able to buy time and create roadblocks for the foreclosing party through a motion to dismiss for failure to effect good service. Such a defense is not unique to foreclosure, and may be raised in any civil litigation matter.

The failure to effect good service is a jurisdictional defect. Jurisdictional defects are often fatal to a judgment rendered before the defect has been cured. Importantly, entire judgments for foreclosure have been overturned on appeal where the defendant alleged failure to effect good service. See *Silva v. BAC*

Home Loans Servicing, L.P., 60 So.3d 555 (Fla. App. 2011) (reversing default judgment based on lack of valid service); *Ciolli v. City of Palm Bay*, 59 So.3d 295 (Fla. App. 2011) (reversing summary judgment based on lack of valid service).

Chapter 13:
Failure to Comply With Discovery

A court may dismiss a foreclosure case if the plaintiff fails to comply with the defendant's discovery requests. This is another defense that is common to a broad spectrum of cases, rather than just foreclosures. In order to use this defense, the defendant need only file a motion that indicates the documents that the plaintiff failed to produce, and request a dismissal of the case. If a lender or servicer plaintiff in a foreclosure action is unable to comply with discovery demands, the court may dismiss the matter. See, e.g., *U.S. Bank National Association v. Harpster*, Case No. 51-2007-CA-6684ES (Fl. Cir. Ct. 2010).

These motions are typically made under an applicable state statute requiring all parties to comply with the rules or order of any court. Additionally, case law typically provides courts with the inherent power to impose dismissal where a party fails to comply with its rules or orders. See, e.g., *Lasley v. Cushing*, 244 So. 2d 770 (Fla. 1st DCA 1971).

Chapter 14:
Federal Claims and Defenses

Truth in Lending Act of 1968 (TILA)

The Truth in Lending Act (TILA) is a federal law that requires disclosure of the terms and cost of obtaining consumer credit. Regulation Z is the implementing code. TILA applies to consumer credit transactions that are secured by the consumer's principal dwelling but does not apply to the original mortgage on a consumer's residential home. The intent of TILA is to promote the informed use of consumer credit and address the problem of predatory lending to high-risk borrowers. TILA accomplishes this by setting standards for calculating the cost of consumer credit and standardizing how information is presented to consumers.

Regardless of whether a violation occurred, rescission is available to all borrowers within 3 days after accepting a home equity line of credit. However, if the creditor fails to make material disclosures, the right to rescind may extend up to 3 years. See 15 U.S.C. § 1635(f). Thus, when a failure to disclose is discovered, borrowers may send a written notice of rescission to the lender nullifying the lending agreement. If the court finds a TILA violation and accepts the rescission, the creditor no longer has standing to foreclose.

Usually, TILA violations are raised as counterclaims in a foreclosure action. Although the counterclaim is based on federal law, the case may still be disposed of in state court. Civil remedies permitted in Section 1640 of TILA include actual damages, statutory damages for specific violations (ranging from $100 - $2,000), court costs, attorneys fees, the total of all fees and finance charges paid, and the right to rescission. In practice, demonstrating actual damages is difficult for plaintiffs in many jurisdictions. See e.g., *In re Boganski*, 322 B.R. 422 (9th Cir. BAP 2005) (holding that the plaintiff must prove he would not have accepted the loan if proper disclosures had been made).

Home Ownership and Equity Protection Act of 1994 (HOEPA)

HOEPA, or the Home Ownership and Equity Protection Act, is an amendment to the Truth in Lending Act (TILA). HOEPA targets a specific subset of loans with high fees or costs. Like TILA, the purpose of HOEPA is to counteract abusive lending practices, but HOEPA provides greater consumer protections and greater civil relief.

Under HOEPA, high cost refinance loans are required to follow special disclosure rules. The 2013 HOEPA Rule added supplemental disclosure rules, mandated avoidance of certain loan terms, and included new consumer protections such as homeownership counseling. These changes take effect on January 10, 2014.

HOEPA is a special damages provision to TILA. It is typically raised as a counterclaim in foreclosure actions and may be resolved in state court proceedings. HOEPA damages include repayment of the sum of all fees and finance charges paid by the consumer. HOEPA also affords consumers the opportunity to rescind the transaction up to 3 years later. If a violating lender seeks to foreclose, successful rescission strips the lender of standing. HOEPA also increases the limit for class action damages to the lesser of $1 million dollars or 1%

of the lender's net worth. Ideally, the higher penalties act as disincentives to engage in predatory lending practices.

Real Estate Settlement Procedures Act (RESPA)

The Real Estate Settlement Procedures Act (RESPA) protects homebuyers from abusive practices in the settlement process by requiring disclosure of settlement costs and the applicable interest rate. 12 U.S.C. § 2601. RESPA requires a standardized Good Faith Estimate (GFE) to improve transparency and promote shopping among settlement service providers.

Under RESPA, a lender is prohibited from: accepting kickbacks for referrals to title insurance companies, accepting kickbacks from settlement services companies, and misusing escrow funds. These violations of RESPA all give rise to private causes of action by the consumer and are usually raised as counterclaims in state foreclosure proceedings. Damages for certain violations are defined by statute while others are set at three times the amount of illegal charges plus attorney's fees. Importantly, failure to disclose RESPA-mandated materials to the consumer does not give rise to a private right of action. The statute of limitations for raising RESPA violations is either 1 year or 3 years, depending on the nature of the violation.

Fair Debt Collection Practices Act of 1977 (FDCPA)

The Fair Debt Collection Practices Act (FDCPA), 15 U.S.C. § 1692, seeks to eliminate abusive practices employed in the collection of consumer debt by regulating the business practices of debt collectors. FDCPA applies generally to any third party "debt collector" – a term that is broadly defined by statute. 15 U.S.C. § 1692a. Courts split on whether foreclosure is a form of debt collection regulated under FDCPA. See *Glazer v. Chase Home Finance LLC*, 704 F.3d 453, 459-65 (6th Cir. 2013) (summarizing the split between courts).

Examples of FDCPA violations include: contacting a consumer at his or her workplace regarding a debt, publishing the consumer's information on a bad debt list, and using profane language to harass the consumer. FDCPA also affirmatively mandates that debt collectors identify themselves, provide verification of a debt, and notify the consumer of the right to dispute the debt.

In practice, violations of the FDCPA are often asserted by letter to the collector in an attempt to delay foreclosure proceedings. For instance, if verification of the debt has not been produced to the consumer, the consumer can request verification. While the collector fulfills the request, no collection action may be taken.

Harassed consumers may file suit in state or federal court for violations of FDCPA. Actual and statutory damages may be awarded to prevailing consumers in addition to attorney's fees and costs. Statutory damages are capped at $1,000 per violation. The FDCPA has a 1-year statute of limitations that begins on the date the violation occurred. If the collector has an opportunity to cure the violation, tolling begins on the last day the collector could have complied with FDCPA. Increasingly, it is the attorneys pursuing foreclosure who unwittingly breach FDCPA rules. See e.g., *Shoup v. McCurdy & Candler*, Case No. 1:09-CV-02598 (N.D. Ga. 2009); *Bourff v. Rubin Lublin*, Case No. 1:09-CV-2437 (N.D. Ga. 2009).

Fair Housing Act of 1968 (FHA)

Title VIII of the Civil Rights Act of 1968 is referred to as the Fair Housing Act (FHA). 42 U.S.C. § 3605. The Act prohibits discrimination based on a person's race, religion, national origin, gender, familial status or disability in obtaining finance for housing. Importantly, lenders may discriminate on the basis of ability to pay and credit history.

Violations of the Fair Housing Act may be brought as counterclaims to a foreclosure action or as independent actions. For example, if a lender accelerates or forecloses on a home that houses disabled persons and demonstrates discriminatory intent in doing so, the borrower could claim an FHA violation. When analyzing Fair Housing violations, courts look for: (1) the exercise of discriminatory intent; (2) actions that caused a "disparate impact"; or (3) failures to make reasonable accommodation. *WHEDA v. Tri-Corp Housing*, 2010AP1443 (Wis. Ct. App. 2011).

An aggrieved party may assert a Fair Housing violation in state or federal court. Potential recovery includes actual and punitive damages, attorney's fees and costs, and injunctive relief. Injunctive relief can prohibit the acceleration of the loan or foreclosure depending on circumstances. In the event the U.S. Attorney brings the action representing the public interest, a first time penalty of $50,000 may be assessed and this limit increases to $10,000 for subsequent violations.

Home Affordable Modification Program (HAMP)

HAMP, or the Home Affordable Modification Program, is a means for the lender and borrower to avoid foreclosure actions. It is a federal program that helps sets up loan modifications for eligible homeowners. Loan servicers who enroll in the program must review all mortgages in default or at risk of default under HAMP standards before commencing a foreclosure action. The loan servicer must offer a HAMP modification if the homeowner qualifies. A homeowner may apply for a HAMP modification in order to stay foreclosure proceedings.

HAMP has a trial period where the homeowner's initial compliance in making reduced payments is tested. The defense of promissory estoppel arises where the homeowner successfully complies during the trial period but the loan servicer refuses to make the modification permanent and forecloses instead. The lender's reneging on the promised permanent modification undermines the borrower's reasonable expectation of avoiding foreclosure. These acts form the basis for a promissory estoppel defense.

The lender's improper handling of a HAMP application may also be asserted as an affirmative defense. Foreclosure proceedings may be delayed until the servicer can show it complied with HAMP requirements. If the borrower qualifies for a HAMP modification, the foreclosure process is suspended.

Servicers who participate in the HAMP program receive incentive payments for doing so from the US government. To determine whether a servicer participates in HAMP, one can either contact the servicer to ask or use the government website here: http://tinyurl.com/hamplookup.

Service Members Civil Relief Act (SCRA)

The Service Members Civil Relief Act (SCRA) provides service members, Reservists, and National Guard with protections from lawsuits regarding their financial obligations while on active duty and for a period of time thereafter. This includes actions such as foreclosure. The purpose of the Act is to enable military personnel to commit their full attention to service while on active duty.

During any period of active duty and for nine months after, SCRA requires that a lender obtain a court order before proceeding with a foreclosure. This is true even in non-judicial foreclosure states. A service member can stay foreclosure proceedings or request modification of the loan if the failure to make payments was due to his or her active service. While the Act does not apply if the borrower was on active duty when the loan was taken out, borrowers wishing to engender the sympathy of the court may raise it liberally.

Interestingly, no private right of action is specifically outlined in SCRA. While most federal courts have found a private right exists, the Supreme Court has yet to decide the issue.

Protecting Tenants at Foreclosure Act of 2009 (PTFA)

The Protecting Tenants at Foreclosure Act (PTFA) addressed the problem of renters being evicted when their landlord was foreclosed upon. Under PTFA, renters living in a foreclosed home may continue to rent until the end of their lease or, in the case of month-to-month renters, 90 days. Crucially, the Act does not preempt any state legislation that is more generous to tenants. The time limits set by PTFA may just be a starting point if state law gives the tenant more time.

One practical effect of the Act is that lenders have less incentive to pursue speedy foreclosure because they must wait for a tenant's lease to terminate. The tenant may use a violation of PTFA as an affirmative defense to eviction. (Tenants are named as defendants to foreclosure actions because their rights are being adjudicated in the case as well.) Otherwise, however, PFTA creates no private right of action for tenants – it is merely a protective measure.

Chapter 15:
Defending Through Bankruptcy

Unlike foreclosures, which are governed by state law, bankruptcy proceedings are governed by federal law (11 U.S.C. §§ 101, et seq.) and take place in specialized federal bankruptcy courts. There are 3 types of bankruptcies relevant here – Chapter 7 (liquidation), Chapter 11 (reorganization) and Chapter 13 (wage earner case).

For foreclosure actions, the critical difference between Chapter 7 cases, on the one hand, and Chapter 11 and 13 cases, on the other, is the bankruptcy filing's effect on mortgage debt. Chapter 11 and 13 cases restructure the debtor/borrower's finances with the goal of giving the debtor/borrower a second chance at keeping his home and getting his finances back in order. In those cases, if the debtor/borrower follows his bankruptcy plan by making his payments, his loan will be deemed to be current and the debtor/borrower will keep his home. Chapter 7 is a liquidation proceeding used usually where there is no equity in the home and the debtor is hopelessly behind on the mortgage. The debtor typically will surrender the home and be discharged from all obligations including liability on any mortgage balance. The lender may still foreclose upon the collateralized real estate but cannot pursue the borrower personally for any deficiency.

The effect of a bankruptcy on foreclosure proceedings also depends on timing – whether the borrower files for bankruptcy during or after foreclosure. If the borrower files for bankruptcy (either Chapter 7, 11 or 13) during the foreclosure proceedings but prior to a sale, an automatic stay of the foreclosure proceedings immediately goes into effect by operation of law upon filing a bankruptcy petition. The automatic stay is a powerful injunction that prevents further action by the foreclosure plaintiff and requires the plaintiff to obtain approval of the bankruptcy court to proceed with foreclosure. During bankruptcy, however, typically the debtor/borrower resumes mortgage payments, and the bankruptcy court will not lift the stay so long as those payments continue.

Once the bankruptcy court approves of a Chapter 11 or Chapter 13 plan, so long as it provides that the borrower will pay off the arrears due the lender, the lender is bound by the plan and cannot continue with the foreclosure so long as payments are made.

Filing for bankruptcy during foreclosure proceedings also provides more mortgage modification options for the homeowner. For example, in a Chapter 13 bankruptcy, mortgage arrears are typically spread out over a multi-year period in order to enable the borrower in to bring the loan current. In addition, if the house is underwater, secondary mortgage liens can be stripped or crammed down (i.e., reduced or modified to the value of the equity) and reclassified as unsecured debt thus providing a debtor with further financial relief. Finally, several bankruptcy courts have established litigation modification programs that are available to all debtors (but typically used by Chapter 13 debtors) to enable them to negotiate the terms of a loan modification with their lender under the bankruptcy court's auspices.

Finally, if the borrower files for bankruptcy after the property is foreclosed upon in a judicial foreclosure or "transferred" pursuant to a power-of-sale foreclosure, then that property would not be part of the bankruptcy estate.[3] This will affect any deficiency judgment resulting from the pre-bankruptcy foreclosure action. In a Chapter 7, the deficiency judgment claim will be discharged while, in a Chapter 13, the claim will be relegated to the class of unsecured creditors to be treated under the debtor's plan.

---

[3] There are cases where a debtor can stay the transfer of the property if issues exist regarding the propriety of the sale such as a sale that violates the automatic stay.

Chapter 16:
Failed Defenses

There are a few defenses that are worth noting just as having been tried and, thus far, failed. The first is violation of the pooling and servicing agreement, which cannot serve as a defense to a foreclosure action. The second is a challenge to who owns the note.

As to servicing agreement violations, after a borrower and lender execute a mortgage agreement, it is common for the lender to bundle numerous similar mortgages together and sell them as an investment to another organization. This process is known as mortgage securitization. The new owner of the mortgages, commonly a trust, can then hire a service provider to collect the mortgage payments and do whatever else is necessary to service the loan. The rights and obligations of the parties involved in this entire process are outlined in a pooling and servicing agreement.

It is possible for a trust or service provider to violate a pooling and service agreement. However, a borrower is not a party or third party beneficiary to the agreement, so he generally cannot use the violation as a defense to foreclosure. Further, such a borrower would lack standing to challenge the validity of a mortgage securitization or the loan assignment due to violations of the pooling and servicing agreement.

As to challenging who owns the note, most defenses to foreclosure are premised on the argument that the plaintiff lacks standing to foreclose the mortgage. However, a plaintiff does not need to be the owner of the mortgage note in order to have standing to foreclose. The right to enforce the mortgage can be separated from ownership and given to a service provider. If the plaintiff is a service provider with the right to enforce the mortgage note, an argument that he lacks standing because he is a non-owner will fail in court.

Part Three:
Foreclosure Appeals

A judgment of foreclosure is considered to be a final judgment, so the resulting appeal is a matter of right. This means that the appellate court is guaranteed to hear the appeal and cannot deny permission for such an appeal. However, state law provides strict procedural rules that a party must follow when filing for appeal. Generally, these include strict deadlines for filing the notice of appeal with the trial level court and appellate briefs with the appellate court. A notice of appeal notifies the court and other parties that one party wishes to have an appellate court review the lower court's decision.

In most foreclosure cases, there will be two opportunities to file an appeal. The first opportunity occurs after the entry of the judgment for foreclosure, the second after the entry of the order confirming the foreclosure sale. After the entry of each of these orders, the borrower has a set amount of time to appeal the applicable order, either the judgment of foreclosure or the order confirming the sale. State law will, of course, determine the exact appellate procedure for any given case.

The states have differing rules concerning when a borrower can appeal in a foreclosure case; the appeals clock may start ticking immediately upon entry of the judgment of foreclosure, as in Wisconsin, or the entry of order confirming the sheriff sale may start the clock ticking and an appeal of the judgment may be made after that point. Ohio courts are reputedly split between those that allow a borrower to appeal a judgment of foreclosure after the foreclosure sale has occurred (*U.S. Bank N.A. v. Mobile Associates National Network Systems, Inc.*, 195 Ohio App. 3d 699 (10th Dist. 2011) and those that do not (*Charter Ohio Bank, F.S.B. v. Mysyk*, 2004 Ohio 4391 (11th Dist.)

Despite the pendency of an appeal, trial courts will generally continue with the foreclosure process. This means the post-judgment redemption period will continue to toll, the sheriff sale will proceed as scheduled, and the trial court will ultimately hold a confirmation hearing on the sale. It is worth noting, however, that there are limited instances in which a plaintiff's right to repossess may be infringed upon by a pending appeal. In Arizona, for example, a tenant facing eviction has a statutory right to possession if the tenant files an appeal and posts sufficient bond to cover the rental value of the property pending appeal. *Grady v. Superior Court of Maricopa County*, Case No. CV-2012-01690 (Ariz. Ct. App. 2013).

An interested party will also have an opportunity to appeal the court order confirming the foreclosure sale. In Wisconsin and many states with judicial foreclosures, this appeal is also a matter of right. Unfortunately, enforcement of the confirmation of sale is not usually stayed, even if the confirmation of sale order is appealed. In both the cases of appeal from a judgment of foreclosure and appeal from a confirmation of sale order, the appellant generally has to request and be granted a stay of the underlying matter in order for prosecution or enforcement to stop.

Many of the issues raised on appeal in a foreclosure case are the same or similar to the defenses that a party would argue at trial. A large number of appellate cases center on the issue of standing. In *Deutsche Bank Nat'l Trust Co. v. Mitchell*, 422 N.J.Super. 214, 27 A.3d 1229 (N.J. Super., 2011), the Superior Court of New Jersey reversed a judgment of foreclosure, because "Deutsche Bank did not prove it had standing at the time it filed the original complaint." In that case, the plaintiff filed its complaint a day before it was assigned the note, amending it later. However, the court found that the plaintiff lacked standing at the time the complaint was filed and could not later acquire standing through amending the complaint. Note that this would not stop Deutsche Bank from coming back later and refiling the action for foreclosure, but it restarts the clock and gives the borrower a lot more time.

In *Deutsche Bank Trust Co. Am. v. Angeles*, 428 N.J.Super. 315, 53 A.3d 673 (N.J. Super., 2012), the Superior Court of New Jersey held that a lower court did not abuse its discretion when it refused to grant the defendant equitable relief from a default judgment. The defendant had sought relief under New Jersey rules that allowed relief from judgment if a judgment was void for lack of standing. However, the court found the defendant failed to bring the motion within a reasonable time, when he waited two years after default judgment to raise the standing issue or contest the complaint. While this decision partially rests on interpretation of New Jersey rules, similar statutes exist in other states for relief from default judgment.

In *Kim v. JPMorgan Chase Bank, NA*, 493 Mich. 98, 825 N.W.2d 329 (2012), the Michigan Supreme Court held a foreclosure by advertisement voidable, because it failed to comply with Michigan statutory recording requirements. After Washington Mutual experienced the largest bank failure in American history, JPMorgan purchased its mortgages through a voluntary purchase agreement with the FDIC. The court found that mortgages acquired in such a manner were not acquired by operation of law. As a result,

Michigan law required JPMorgan to record the mortgages before initiating a foreclosure by advertisement. JPMorgan had not done so, so the court held the foreclosure was void.

In *Niday v. GMAC*, 353 Or. 648, 302 P.3d 444 (2013), the Oregon Supreme Court affirmed an appellate court holding that MERS was not a beneficiary of the deed of trust for the purposes of Oregon law on nonjudicial foreclosures. However, the Court also found that MERS could have maintained authority to foreclose if it had provided evidence of an agency relationship with the financial firms, which it hadn't.

In *Garrett v. ReconTrust Company*, Case No. 12-4060 (10th Cir. 2013), the Tenth Circuit held that under federal banking laws and regulations, the laws of the state where a national bank is located are applied to foreclosure sales, not the laws of the state where the property is located. The plaintiff ReconTrust was located in Texas, so Texas law was applied to the Utah foreclosure. As a result, the defendant's arguments based on Utah law did not apply. There is a good possibility this case will be appealed to the US Supreme Court.

In *Bank of America N.A. v. George Minkov*, 2013 WI App 115 (2013), the Wisconsin Court of Appeals reversed an order of summary judgment for foreclosure because Bank of America failed to establish a prima facia case for summary judgment. In support of its decision, the court concluded the following:

(1) The copy of a promissory note was insufficient to establish a prima facie case that Bank of America possessed the original note; and

(2) The plaintiff's employee's affidavit did not demonstrate the personal knowledge necessary for additional documents to be admissible as records of regularly conducted activity.

This case could have important implications in future Wisconsin foreclosure cases where financial institutions have limited proof to support motions for summary judgment.

In *Focht v. Wells Fargo Bank*, N.A. Case Nos. 2D11-4511, 2D11-4980 (Fla. Ct. App. 2013), a Florida appellate court reversed a summary judgment of foreclosure because it found that a genuine issue of material fact existed regarding whether Wells Fargo had standing to foreclose the mortgage. The court also certified the following question to the state supreme court:

Can a plaintiff in a foreclosure action cure the inability to prove standing at the inception of suit by proof that the plaintiff has since acquired standing?

A decision on this question could have had broad implications on foreclosure defense in Florida; however, Wells Fargo has not filed documents to pursue the appeal. It is possible that Wells Fargo did not want the question conclusively answered because an answer in the negative would hurt their position moving forward.

These appeals all involved appeals of the judgment of foreclosure but, as discussed, it is also possible to appeal the order confirming the foreclosure sale. Potential grounds for appealing this order include that the notice of the sale was insufficient to comply with state law on foreclosure sales, or that the property was not sold for fair value. Note that fair value is not the same as fair market value. For the purposes of confirmation of foreclosure, fair value is a price that is not so low that it "shocks the conscience of the court." Courts are not easily shocked, however, because it is possible for a property to be sold for nearly half of its fair market value and still have that be considered fair value for the purposes of a foreclosure sale. Overturning of the confirmation of sale has worked in cases where the court did not make an adequate finding on fair value, or where the sale price was inadequate, usually closer to the 50% of fair market value mark, or there was an irregularity in procedure.

It is worth noting that an appeal of a confirmation of foreclosure sale appeals just that – the sale, not the underlying judgment. In many states including Wisconsin, an appeal of a foreclosure sale is not a forum where appellants are welcome to protest regarding the judgment itself. Accordingly, if the appeal is successful, it typically puts the case back to the place it was in before the sale occurred. While not impossible in every jurisdiction, such an appeal would not typically have an impact on the judgment of foreclosure itself.

Obviously, the breadth of foreclosure appeals is limited only by the panoply of legal issues that arise in the context of foreclosure litigation. Further, the procedural peculiarities of each individual jurisdiction will heavily influence what potentially meritorious issues are available for appellant.

Appendix One:
General Resources for Borrowers

The following are external resources so, while not written by the author of this book, may be helpful to anyone wishing to familiarize himself with the foreclosure process and various alternatives to foreclosure.

Foreclosure Terminology

Talking about foreclosure real estate can be hard enough without even entering the market. That's because foreclosures tend to have their own language, employing many obscure words originating in government housing legislation and real estate law. Without a background in these areas, prospective investors won't be able to decipher even the simplest foreclosure contract. This article lists some of the more common foreclosure-related terms as a reference for people interested in this lucrative market.

Abandonment: Wherein a property owner has given up ownership rights without coercion, and does not want to retrieve those rights, or pass them to somebody else. A situation involving an unused property does not guarantee abandonment.

Acceleration Clause: A clause commonly written in a mortgage enabling the lender to demand full repayment immediately, rather than at the end of the contracted term. The clause must also detail an occurrence that would put it into effect, such as a default on regular payments, sale of the property, or reassignment of property rights. In most cases the debtor must be given reasonable notice, and a chance to reverse the occurrence. The debtor is also immune from acceleration if there is no such clause written into the agreement.

Chattel: Personal property, including household items.

Closing Costs: Expenses not related to the marketing and selling of the property, sure as loan fees and paperwork fees. Foreclosures might also involve extra legal and escrow fees.

Deed in Lieu of Foreclosure: Property owners may deed their property to the lender if foreclosure is imminent, rather than go through the entire process. For the deeding to be official, the lender must give approval.

Default: Failure of the borrower to make payments as required by the lender. "Default" may refer to a missed payment without any further repercussion, or a series of missed payments resulting in a failed mortgage.

Equity Right of Redemption: The right of the borrower to remove all encumbrances related to the mortgage, in order to avoid foreclosure.

Federal Housing Administration (FHA): A part of the Housing and Urban Development Federal agency responsible for determining industry standards for mortgage loans by private lenders. FHA also insures mortgages by private lenders. Foreclosure investors must occasionally deal with this agency.

Federal National Mortgage Association: Also known as FNMA, or Fannie Mae, this federal agency oversees conventional residential mortgages, and will buy out loans that follow its rules. Some foreclosure investments require direct communication with this agency.

HUD1 Statement: A form mandated by the US Department of Housing and Urban Development that specifies the costs of acquiring a foreclosed home.

Loan-To-Value Ratio: A comparison of the total loan amount and the lesser of the property's sale price or appraised value.

Notice of Rescission: A notice from the lender notifying the borrower that he or she is again in good standing with the loan, and payment deficiencies have been corrected.

Short Sale: A property sale priced at or below market value, and lower than the amount of a mortgage on the same property.

Truth-in-Lending Act: A law requiring the lender to provide the borrower with a full written explanation of the mortgage's terms.

Alternatives to Foreclosure

A delay in payment can have very serious consequences for your mortgage situation. If the delinquency in payments has become too severe then your home could be in danger of foreclosure. A foreclosure means that the lending institution that gave you your mortgage will repossess your property.

The time that you have to negotiate a deal is often very limited. In most states, a borrower that is in default 60 or more days is just about out of time. This period varies from state to state so make sure that you have checked your local laws. Lenders can and will take legal action to foreclosure on your home if you are not talking to them.

Here are some possible solutions that you can offer to the lender to avoid foreclosure. While not all will be satisfactory to the lender, you can at least make the offer and let them tell you.

Paying the delinquency (curing and reinstating the loan).

Generally, all lending institutions are required to accept all the payments that were delinquent and reinstate the loan. The amount that you have to pay may also include some legal fees especially if you are already in the foreclosure stage. There are also lending institutions that require certified funds in order to reinstate the loan. The lender may require that everything that is owed be paid in one lump sum. However, sometimes lenders will allow a repayment plan. Repayment plans require higher payments than the regular monthly mortgage amount for a period of time until the loan is brought up-to-date.

Reduced Payments.

Lenders may be willing to take a reduced payment for a specific period (6 months, for instance), which would allow you to remain in the home and catch up the default amount later on. Some lenders will not allow you to do this, but it never hurts to try. In the meanwhile, reduce your expenses, pick up another job and somehow create another source of income. This may be all that you need to protect your home and avoid foreclosure. Reducing your expenses is a priority. Cut the cable bill, cancel memberships and shop with coupons. Reducing your monthly expenses by only a few hundred dollars a month may be the answer to getting back on track. Even a small reduction in monthly expenses or increase in monthly income, in combination with reduced payments, will likely get you back on track.

Short Sale.

Lenders may let you sell the property for less then what they are owed on the loan. More and more lenders are allowing this type of transaction as they have realized that it costs them much more to pursue the foreclosure then if they just settle and take what they can get.

Payment Deferment.

Some lenders may allow you to defer a payment or two, they tack the payments on the end of the loan and allow you time to catch up and stay current. This option is only just now beginning to become available as lenders are doing whatever they can to help avoid the foreclosure process.

Forbearance and Repayment.

One of the most common ways of resolving a delinquent mortgage is to work out a plan with your lending institution where in you get to pay a part of your delinquency every month on top of your regular monthly payments. If you are in a situation where you are not able to meet the monthly mortgage payments, your lender can elect to extend the forbearance by lowering or even suspending payments altogether for a certain period of time up until you can start a repayment schedule. Forbearance arrangements are typically given when there are external circumstances that promise to be remedied, such as a temporary loss of employment.

Loan Modification.

A loan modification involves changing one or more terms of a mortgage. Modifications can be considered to reduce the interest rate of the mortgage, change the mortgage product (from an adjustable rate to a fixed rate, for example), extend the term of the mortgage or capitalize delinquent payments (add delinquent payments to the mortgage balance-only available in extreme hardship situations).

Payment Assistance.

Some state and local governments and also private charitable organizations have instituted programs that help people with delinquencies pay all or part of their mortgage obligation for a certain period of time.

Reamortization.

In a reamortization, the delinquent mortgage amount is added to the loan balance as a way of bringing the mortgage payments up to date. This move increases not only the total loan amount but also the monthly payments. Of course, the increase in payment will not be as large if the life of the loan is also extended. This is another form of curing/reinstating the loan.

Private sale.

A private sale of the property affected by the delinquency can also be done as, if the property has a positive equity balance, it will allow you to meet your obligations as well as get any equity that may have accumulated. In private sales (that aren't short sales), the sale amount must greater than the stated amount owed on the loan.

The primary goal of a private sale is to recoup 100% of the equity minus selling costs. Unfortunately, many homeowners get caught up in the emotions of the hardship and overlook the realities of their financial circumstances. Almost as if with blinders on, they stagger about hoping for a magic solution, sometimes waiting until it is to late to come up with a rational plan. If a homeowner can reasonably assess their finances and determine that they cannot carry the financial load, they might be much better off selling the property and preserving the bulk of their equity until they are again able to become homeowners, if they so wish. They must act quickly so that their credit is not ruined by the failure to make their mortgage payments on time. Further, once the loan goes delinquent and into foreclosure status, the outstanding balance on the loan will increase rapidly, due in no small part to the added late fees and legal fees. This means that the equity is getting eaten up by the bank and the bank's lawyers. If it's at all an option, even if you have to sell it for less than you think it's worth, if it's more than the balance on the loan, it's worth doing so to avoid foreclosure. If you can sell the home for more than the balance on the loan, then you preserve the most important or valuable part, namely the equity.

Lease Purchase Agreement.

This option involves finding a tenant to lease your home from you, with an option to purchase the home at the end to the agreed period or time, usually 12 to 24 months. You set a price for them to buy the house when the agreement is signed; this will allow you to save the equity and buy some time to recover. With a tenant that has the option to buy your home you may be able to increase the monthly payment from what a tenant would pay so hopefully make the monthly mortgage payment, receive a one-time up-front non-refundable payment of 1-3%, locate non-traditional buyers, and avoid foreclosure.

Deed-in-Lieu.

A Deed in Lieu is an option in which a borrower voluntarily deeds collateral property back to the bank in exchange for a release from all obligations under the mortgage.

File for Bankruptcy.

There are two chapters dealing with personal bankruptcy: Chapter 13 and Chapter 7. The main difference between the two chapters is that Chapter 13 helps individual debtors pay off their debt with court supervision and protection while Chapter 7 eliminates, or in legal terms, liquidates, the debtor's debt. Based on this simplistic definition alone bankruptcy may seem like the simplest and best solution to your financial problems. However, when considering filing bankruptcy, be aware that it is not an action that simply frees you from your debt, it is a complex legal process that has weighty financial consequences. For most debtors, it is not the best option and should be considered as a last resort after all other options have been investigated or attempted. Individual financial circumstances are so different that you should seek the counsel of a financial planner or accountant and a bankruptcy attorney in order to discuss your particular financial situation and the implications of a bankruptcy. If you do not have an established relationship with an attorney, I would recommend that you get two or three opinions. Most bankruptcy attorneys offer free consultations to determine eligibility.

Most of these alternatives presume that you will be able to pay your mortgage payments at some point.

But there is also a particular foreclosure alternative called a loss mitigation program. The federal government as well as the mortgage industry established this type of program as a way of stopping foreclosures. Under this program you are given options that will not only assist you in keeping your home even if you do not have the financial capability to pay for the mortgage payments. With these types of programs, it becomes so much easier to address the problem of foreclosures.

Loan Modifications

Loan modifications are becoming more and more common with the rising foreclosure rates in the United States. Until recently, mortgage companies have been reluctant to provide help to people facing foreclosures by utilizing mortgage modification programs. Lenders are now using these solutions more often because of the huge influx in homeowners that are in jeopardy of losing their home to a foreclosure. The lenders have come to realize that by working with the homeowners they have a chance at avoiding additional loses that are putting many mortgage companies into bankruptcy.

A mortgage modification or often times called a loan modification allows borrowers the opportunity to re-negotiate the terms of their mortgage loans, thereby reducing the required monthly payment. This option gives people facing a financial hardship the chance to save their home from a foreclosure. Establishing a new payment plan through a successful mortgage modification will help you avoid foreclosure.

Lenders and borrowers have many reasons to work through avoiding foreclosure together, and establish a suitable plan that works for all parties involved. Selling your home may not be an option, especially with current market conditions and the circumstances that have caused this unfortunate situation to begin with. Therefore, if your home is to be saved from foreclosure, you and your lender will have to work together.

Mortgage modifications are often times a reasonable solution to prevent foreclosure. By negotiating a new payment, lenders still get their money and the borrower is able to keep their home. However, negotiating a mortgage modification is not always simple. Successful loan modification will require documentation to prove your current financial position with the lender. This information is also used to verify your ability to pay the new loan amount, should a modification be granted.

While not all banks offer this type of solution, it never hurts to talk to them and find out. It may be just what you need to prevent losing your home to a foreclosure. Lenders are starting to work more with borrowers facing foreclosure in this difficult time. Lenders do not want your home, they are in the business of lending money not property management, and with the close to 2 million homes in foreclosure lenders are running out of options, too. Qualifying for a loan modification may be difficult and time consuming, but keep in mind what your goal is. Protect your most valuable asset and save your home from foreclosure with a mortgage loan modification.

[Author's note: Loan modifications are the single most common way we help our borrower defendant clients out of foreclosure. While, in theory, a borrower should be able to negotiate a loan modification with the lender or servicer directly, this is not how it works in practice. I cannot overstate how often clients come to us having already applied for a loan modification, yet are nonetheless in foreclosure. Once we get involved, we cooperate with the plaintiff's attorney directly. We request a mediator to work with the servicer or lender, and we apply for another loan modification. Only then do the servicers or lenders see fit to offer the client a modification. There is a communication gap between lenders and borrowers that attorneys and mediators are often able to help solve, rendering loan modifications (even if previously denied) an accessible solution.]

Negotiating With Your Lender

The lender should always work with a borrower if the borrower takes the initiative to communicate any financial hardships that may have caused the default. Negotiate with the lender for a payment adjustment in order to make up for the missed payment or payments. It is imperative that you act quickly in order to prevent the sale of your home, because once the foreclosure process begins you have a limited time before your house is sold. Contact your lender to explain your situation and work out a way for you to keep your house. You have the most time and the best chance of being able to negotiate a solution before the trustee files the notice of default. If foreclosure has already begun you should work with counsel to contact the lender immediately.

One of the most common causes of failure to communicate is that many homeowners facing foreclosure avoid contacting their lenders because they are upset or embarrassed. Many times the homeowner mistakenly believes the lender will not help them because they feel that the lender prefers to foreclose. In reality, the opposite is true. Banks and other lenders are primarily in the business of earning money by collecting interest on loans that they have made. Having a specific process in place in order to invest and receive the interest payments derives their income. They find it cumbersome to go through the foreclosure process, and usually are not well equipped to manage foreclosed properties. Because of this, most lenders are willing to work with homeowners because foreclosure is more costly for them. It forces them to allocate time and resources to an unprofitable activity. Contact your lender immediately! Do not ignore phone calls and letters from your lender. If you do not inform your lender of your situation, it will be will assumed that you do not intend to pay and the process will go forward.

It is important to prepare well before you contact your lender. You must gather all documents supporting your income and expenses, as well as all loan account information. When you call ask to speak to someone in the customer service department, be upfront about your circumstances and be prepared to discuss your financial situation in detail. Your lender needs to know clearly your financial situation in order to determine whether they are able to offer a solution.

If you are uncomfortable with negotiating with your lender by yourself or if you want to better understand what options you have, contact a *reputable* foreclosure assistance-counseling agency. When selecting an agency to work with, choose one from the U.S. Department of Housing and Urban Development's list of approved housing counseling agencies. Beware of phony "counseling agencies" that approach you with the promise to advise you on your situation, provided that you pay a large fee! Similarly, counseling agencies may advertise on television, but they are generally not as good of an option as a diligent attorney.

[Author's note: It is distressing how many times clients come in having paid $3,000 or so to some counseling service that kind of seems like a law firm or similar, usually located on the west coast or in Florida, that turned out to be a total scam. The services pop up and disappear so quickly that even the Internet consumer reports and Better Business Bureau can't keep up with them. Sometimes, clients think that the agency (sometimes even called the "Whatever Law Firm") will represent them in an existing foreclosure action. When the agency never appears on their behalf, the clients may in turn face a default judgment, and the timeline for appeal may even pass. So don't answer any television commercials or solicitations in the mail for these foreclosure assistance agencies. You don't need to pay some out of state company thousands of dollars to

negotiate a loan modification for you. It's distressing because the money is often altogether lost, but the lesson is to not believe the nice people on the phone from California or Florida or Washington State who say they can help you with your mortgage in Wisconsin. Rather, consult a qualified foreclosure attorney in your local area. Someone to whom you have been referred by a friend or another lawyer is ideal.]

Read all communications from your lender.

Time is your enemy, so the earlier the potential problem is recognized by both parties, the better the chances of a resolution. If you are suffering from financial loss due to the death or loss of a spouse, illness, or unexpected increase in your outgoings, contact the lender and request a loan modification, which effectively changes the terms of the loan to lower the payments. This is a very common process, but you will need to offer evidence about the change in your circumstances. If you feel that you are qualified for a loan modification, and your lender refuses, contact the Housing and Urban Development (HUD) office for advice. Get in touch with your lender and request forbearance if your loss of income is temporary. This means that you may get a period that is granted during which your monthly payments are "suspended." After which you must resume your monthly payments with a partial payment in addition towards the payments you missed.

Always be honest and upfront with the lender and they will work with you. After examining your financial position and the reason for your nonpayment, the lender could reduce the monthly payment or suspend payments temporarily. Be honest with your lender and by working with them and examining the options available, as it is possible to get the financial help to stop foreclosure. Foreclosures cost lenders money, big money, so it is in their interests to reach a workout with the borrower, either to rescue the mortgage, if this is possible, or to reduce the loss as a result of foreclosure. Don't be intimidated by the lender or his attorneys. Apprise yourself of your exact financial position. Know your rights as well as options and be honest in your statements. Maintain a written record of all communications.

[Author's Note. While in principle the author agrees that foreclosures generally costs banks a lot of money and should therefore be disfavored, in practice this is not always the case. Lenders often do not have the administrative capacity to assist homeowners who are in financial trouble. While no individual lender or servicer employee who a borrower gets on the phone is out to "get them," lenders and banks undergo a sort of corporate incapacity. Many borrowers report that no one person ever seems to know what's going on with their file, or that they've been told one thing and something else entirely has occurred, or that they were misadvised or misinformed. Accordingly, while in a perfect world the banks

and lenders would be competent and coherent and easy to communicate with, always approach promises of concessions with caution. Just because the agent says a foreclosure action won't be filed while they try to sort out a loan modification doesn't mean it's true. If you ever aren't paying your mortgage, always put the money you should be paying in a separate earmarked account. When the piper comes round to be paid, you will be ready.]

Borrowing Money to Get On Track

Sometimes the only way to get back on track and reinstate your mortgage is to pay a lump sum to the bank to cure the arrears and outstanding fees due. Several options exist for borrowing money to do so.

Borrow money from family or friends.

Many people tend to shy away from this as their first option. One would think that this option would be the most common-sense place to start. Many people completely eliminate this as a means to gather the funds necessary to bring the loan current simply because they are embarrassed to ask. They do not want family or friends to know that they have encountered financial difficulties, so they look elsewhere. Family or friends many times are the ones that are most committed to lending a helping hand. If they are able, they may be willing to help out. Oftentimes because of embarrassment, they are not approached until it is too late in the foreclosure process, and are unable to obtain funds quickly enough to help out. Obviously, there are situations where the family members or friends are not approached because there are already strained relations, or borrowers want to avoid causing any discomfort to their inner circle of friends or family.

Approach the request for assistance in a very businesslike manner. Look to secure their interest just as you would expect if you were the one providing the funds to someone else in trouble. The greater degree of security that you can offer them in protecting their funds, the greater probability of successfully obtaining the funds necessary to stop the foreclosure.

Borrow from institutional lenders.

Another option is to borrow from institutional lenders to bring up back payments. This can be done by refinancing, or simply by borrowing against the equity in the home. These lenders will primarily consider equity when determining approval of a loan. Equity is defined as the difference between the fair market value of the home and what is owed on the mortgage. Refinancing is when you take out another loan in order to pay off the existing mortgage. When refinancing to avoid foreclosure, you may be able to obtain a lower interest rate, a longer payment period, and/or a lower monthly payment, which would make your mortgage payments more affordable. Usually lenders that become aware that you have fallen behind in the mortgage payments will shy away from lending to you, so if you expect to borrow from an institutional lender, you must act very quickly before your credit reflects any late payments. If the lender is aware that you are in default, they will probably refuse to lend, or offer a loan with a much higher interest rate to account for your previous inability to meet financial obligations.

Borrow from private party lenders.

There are individuals that have funds to invest and are looking for a higher return on their investment than can be obtained by depositing money with savings institutions. These individuals are expecting a high rate of return on their cash investments, and understand that the loan that they are funding is a high-risk loan. Usually, once the homeowner falls behind in their mortgage payments, it is increasingly difficult to borrow money. These private lenders usually consider the equity in the property when making the loan. Because the borrower is behind in their payments, the lender cannot look upon the borrower's ability to repay in a timely manner as the primary basis for qualification. The lender looks for the security of their investment to the ability to recover it based on the property's market value and what is owed by the borrower on the property. Almost without exception, these loans carry a much higher interest rate than the normal home loans obtainable at banks or other lending institutions. They are, however, sometimes the only option left to a homeowner in foreclosure.

Practical Steps to Avoid Foreclosure

With the onset of globalization, there has been a rapid change in our lifestyle. In our busy hectic schedules, we often tend to overlook the need to make proper investments to save money. But chores like this, which may seem trivial, may bring you long-term benefits. But limiting needless spending and trying to earn more money is often not enough. As many research reports have confirmed, in a significant number of foreclosure case the lender did not respond to the mortgage company's call.

A recent research report revealed that 1 out of every 510 households was facing the problem of foreclosures. The drooping real estate scenario clearly bears out the need to save money all the more. The problem of bad loans persists especially for first-time homebuyers.

There is also the problem of mortgage brokers who downplay the seriousness of variable rates in order to increase their own profit margins. So, do not get caught up in the mad frenzy of buying real estate. Make property-buying decisions carefully and conservatively so that you may avoid a future foreclosure. A foreclosure not only means you lose your title to the property, but it will also have an adverse impact on your credit report.

There are several ways to avoid foreclosure and save money as outlined below.

- A lot of dangerous situations can be avoided if you contact your lender as soon as you realize that your payment will be late.
- Never ignore the lender's letters or phone calls. Ignoring the problem will not make it go away.
- Do not try to ignore or shy away from lenders by avoiding their phone calls and letters. This will only aggravate the existing crisis situation. Instead, have a candid discussion with your lender about the cause of and potential solution to your problems.
- Reinstatement is often cited as temporary solution to avoid the problem of foreclosure.

- Last but not the least, you can go for regular counseling programs from financial consultants to avoid the problem of foreclosures.

However, documentation plays a crucial part in avoiding the problem of foreclosure. You should therefore keep handy the following financial details.

- A proper and up to date statement of your current financial circumstances.
- A detailed statement of your current income status.
- A detailed list of household expenses.

If you want to avoid the problem of foreclosure, you should also start saving money right now. Start off with a simple savings bank account and make small but regular contributions so that you have a cushion in a time of crisis. Money does contribute to happiness and eases the stresses of life to a great extent.

It is also critical to take action as early as possible once you realize you are having a problem. This means that you should contact the person or company that holds the title to your property as soon as you think you may be in trouble. It is tempting to avoid the problem to the point of not answering the telephone when those creditors call, but that is not going to solve the issue. In fact, creditors who aren't getting answers or satisfaction are more likely to take action than those with whom you've been talking.

Another reason you should start talking to your creditors well before foreclosure becomes immediate and unavoidable is that you have more options at that point than when the creditor is already taking action. One of those options could be the chance to renegotiate your loan. You might be eligible for a refinancing loan that will stretch your payments out over a longer period of time, meaning you'll have lower monthly payments. That could significantly increase your ability to make those payments on time.

Not only could you be eligible for a longer payoff, you may also qualify for a loan that's larger than your current payoff. That means you could get some cash back from refinancing your loan. If you're having trouble meeting other bills as well because of some short-term issue, this influx of cash could be the answer you're looking for.

If you take time to contact your lender, you may also find it willing to give you a break on a payment or two. Some lenders will allow you to pay the interest due, putting the rest of the payment off until the end of your note. While you probably won't have the option to do this more than once or twice, it could be the answer to short-term problems that sometimes hamper the ability to make payments on time.

It's human nature to avoid confrontations, including those that occur when you've had trouble making your payments on time. But this isn't a situation that's going to resolve itself. Take time to contact your lender. Explain as much of the problem as you can and ask for advice. You'll find them much more willing to negotiate with you early in the process than after you've missed several payments.

[Author's note: As to the last sentence, maybe. Many clients have reported being told by the servicer of the loan that they simply must let the property go into a delinquent status before the servicer or lender will discuss alternatives to foreclosure such as a modification. While this might be true, following this (in my opinion, reckless) advise by the bank has had disastrous outcomes for many. In such instances, early consultation with a qualified foreclosure attorney is critical.]

Protecting Your Home's Value in the Foreclosure Crisis

While home foreclosures are on the rise, there is another side of this economic dilemma. Many investors are targeting foreclosures as profitable investments; unfortunately, this is not good news for most homeowners. Foreclosures are causing property values to decrease therefore reducing the value of homes that are not facing foreclosure. While people like to point out the good things about foreclosure, the key to preventing this from happening across the United States in too a avoid foreclosure in the first place.

Foreclosed homes invite vandals and squatters looking for a place to go that is out of the weather. This spells disaster for neighborhood that has a high rate of foreclosures. Vacant properties will bring trouble and therefore drive property values down.

When lenders try to unload foreclosure properties as quick as they can, in many cases this means that lenders sell the properties at up to 40 - 50% of the market value. Even with properties selling this low, some foreclosures can remain vacant for an extended period. Just because the home is sold does not mean that there is someone moving in, many investors have vacant properties in their portfolio.

Here are a couple things that you can do to help protect the value of your home.

Keep your eyes open.

Keeping watch of the properties in the area that have been foreclosed on will help to keep your neighborhood free of vandals and squatters. Foreclosures are on the rise and thousands of homes a month are going into foreclosure. Keeping your eye on homes in your area will help keep the vandals from stealing appliances, damaging the property and forcing lenders to board up properties. Boarded up properties are invitations to more troubled property values. Lenders will sell homes that have been boarded up for even less, just to move the property. If this happens in your neighborhood, then the value of your own home will suffer. If you are hoping to sell your home before foreclosure, then it is in your best interest to take an active role in managing and taking care of your neighborhood.

Do not sell when you're in a panic.

Home ownership is a long-term investment, and while foreclosures are, on the rise, they will level out and the market will recover at some point. Remain calm and do not panic, now is probably not the time to sell your home especially if you are trying to make a little money. Home values are being driven down; buyers are looking to buy them cheap and below market value right now. In some cases you can still sell your home for a profit as originally planned, do not try to sell just because the local markets are flooded with foreclosures.

Home foreclosures are expected to continue for now, so hang in there, and do not dump your house just because of foreclosures in your area. You bought it as a long-term investment to begin with, and this is a short-term problem. The houses market will recover at some point and your property value will likely rise once again.

Reasons to Avoid Foreclosure

Real estate is not always an easy venture to be involved in. Mortgages are huge loans, and monthly payments can be extremely steep. Especially with the trend a few years back to give out sub-prime mortgages, there have been a lot of foreclosures lately. But foreclosure should be avoided if at all possible in almost all circumstances.

So let's assume for a moment that you are unable to make your mortgage payments. You become a defaulted owner. Now what? Well, typically, your lending institution will foreclose its mortgage. If this happens, not only will you lose your property when it goes back to the bank, you will lose all your equity. In addition, foreclosure reduces your credit rating, leaving a permanent stain on your credit account. This can be extremely hard to remove, and may prevent you from ever borrowing again. Finally, you may even have to pay taxes on the debt reduction amount. So in trying to save money, you've only added another expense to your list of bills. All in all, foreclosure is a bad deal for you.

There are two main types of foreclosure, foreclosure by judicial sale and foreclosure by power of sale. In the former, the court supervises the sale of the property. In the latter, the bank or mortgage holder sells the home. In a strict foreclosure, not in use in all states, the bank would assume the deed of the defaulted mortgage, without the obligation to sell. This method is less popular as few banks want to become landlords. Usually, by whatever means, the foreclosure involves the sale of the property.

If you are unable to make your mortgage payments, or in any other way are unable to fulfill the obligations of your lending contract, it is best if you sell your real estate as soon as possible. This may mean selling at a much lower rate than market value, however as a homeowner, you may be able to retain some equity from your home, and you will definitely save your credit rating. This is very important for your future real estate purchases, and just about anything else in your life. By selling your home yourself, with or without the help of an agent, you are keeping the power in your hands. Even if you come out of it with no equity, the chances of losing money are slim unless your home has become totally derelict. Even then, you are still better off selling it yourself than allowing a foreclosure to go ahead.

While in a stressful situation such as mounting debt, it can seem like the easy thing to drop everything and run. But as I've outlined, it is never to your advantage to let a property foreclose. The key to saving yourself from this fate may be an honest analysis of your expenses. If you can see a problem coming, you have more time to act on it. Rather than waiting to the last minute, put your home up for sale as soon as you suspect you will have trouble making payments in the future. The more time you have to sell, the more likely you'll walk away with a fair price for your property. You may even be able to find another, cheaper home, and nobody will have been the wiser that you narrowly escaped financial disaster.

Pricing Your Home to Sell

If you cannot negotiate a solution with your lender or come up with the money to cure the deficiency, then its usually time to either sell your home, or lay down and let your lender put you out. You need to decide what is the least amount you will take for your home. This isn't some pie in the sky number to come up with; it should be what you owe. That doesn't necessarily mean that this is all you are shooting for, but you need to have an exit strategy in place.

Getting organized deals with collecting comparables because you need to find out what houses in your area are going for. This is easy to do, just jump in your car or take a walk around you neighborhood.

You are looking for realtor signs and "For Sale" or "FSBO" signs with literature about that particular home attached. When you get back from your trip with the info you went after you are going to call local realtors in your area and ask them what homes in your area are going for. The realtor will usually have a list in the MLS that has the most recent homes sold in you area and what the selling price was. If you are internet savvy, of course you can look up this information on a website like Trulia or Zillow.

Make sure you are comparing apples to apples here. If you have a one story three bedrooms with 1 1/2 baths make sure you find the selling prices of similar homes. FYI if the realtor that you call is any good he or she is going to ask a lot of questions. You don't have to tell them your situation but you can if you are comfortable doing so. A kind realtor might just pull comparables for you and give you an idea of what you can sell your property for, fast – and fast is what you need, if foreclosure is looming.

Foreclosure Auctions

Whether you are an investor that would like to get into buying foreclosed homes for your personal use or to flip the property or if you are having your home foreclosed on, you should know what to expect at a foreclosure auction. Of course, the actual steps that will be taken can vary a bit from state to state and from house to house, but it is good to know what you will be getting into when you go to a foreclosure auction. Foreclosure auctions can be exciting, even fun, but knowing what to expect will help you make the most of the experience, whether you are an investor or a homeowner that is trying to get your house back.

Before the Auction

You'll likely find out about the foreclosure auction in a local newspaper and you will probably also be served with papers announcing the sale. You need to think about arrangements for where you are going to move, even if you never considered moving before. You should have an idea of where you can go after you aren't in your home anymore. Now is the time to get aggressive with saving money as you are going to need it, so save as much as you can afford to.

While you do this, potential buyers for your home are researching its history and value. Someone offering to buy your home before it goes to foreclosure auction may contact you. It will be up to you to find a qualified attorney to counsel you as to whether this is a good idea and whether the specific offer you receive would benefit you.

What Happens At the Auction

The auction will typically start with the auctioneer reading legal notices as well as a legal description of the property. The auctioneers will usually then begin taking bids on the property. If the auctioneer has pre-qualified bidders the process is more streamlined, if not, each time a bid is made the auctioneer will then ask for the bidders deposit check, which is typically right around $5,000 for residential auctions. After each bid the auctioneer will attempt to solicit bids for higher amounts. Each auction is different, but the auction increments usually are set by the auctioneer and may be by $100, $500, or $1,000 per bid. The auctioneer will continue to solicit bids by this increment until it is clear that the highest bid has been reached. Then, the auctioneer will announce, "Going once, going twice, three times, sold!" indicating that the auction is over and the property has been sold to the highest bidder.

Once the bidding has ended a foreclosure deed and purchase papers will be drawn up and validated by the new owner or purchaser and the mortgage holder. A grace will likely be given to allow the purchaser to find financing or to come up with the funds to cover the full amount of the bid. This grace period is usually 30 days unless the purchaser and the mortgage holder agree to other terms. After the grace period a closing will take place, so that the new owner can formally take the title to the property.

[Author's note: In some states, such as Wisconsin, the foreclosure sale is not final until it is confirmed by the court in a hearing.]

What Happens, Now?

The purchaser can do what he or she intended to do with the property, whether it is to move into the home or to sell it for full market value. The money paid by the purchaser will be distributed in order of priority, first of which would be taxes. After taxes money will be paid to the mortgage, then the second and third mortgage if applicable. If there is still money after paying these debts, remaining money will be paid to lien holders and creditors. There is a very slim chance that there will be money left over after all of the debts are paid, if this is the case then the monies will be paid to the former home owner.

What about the Original Owner?

The original owner will often be at the auction so that they can bid on their home, and this is legal as long as they have the deposit required. If the owner of the home that has been foreclosed does bid on the home they must remember that the deposit is not refundable and the deposit assumes that they will be able to finance the home within the grace period. Owners must also remember that if they buy the property back old debts may merge and become reinstated such as second and third mortgages that became void when the first mortgage foreclosed on the property unless one has filed bankruptcy and is truly free and clear of these debts. Owners will often drum up the funds to make the deposit so that they can have another 30 days to try to save their home. Owners may or may not be successful in their attempts to save their home at a foreclosure auction.

As you can see, there are a lot of things that go into a foreclosure auction, but none of them are all that difficult to understand, but knowing about them makes the auction less stressful. The auction itself is not all that complicated, but it can be very fast paced. At some foreclosure auctions there are a lot of people, at others there are only a few because of the location or just the debts attached to the property, or even the state of the property.

Foreclosure Crisis Statistics

A recent report released by Mortgage Bankers Association on Mortgage Foreclosure numbers, revealed that, at present, the mortgage market is involved in the most awful foreclosure crisis in the recorded history. It is almost 15 percent of the sub prime borrowers defaulted and the prime borrowers have started to follow suit. During the last few years, many people with the help of easy credit and adjustable rate mortgages bought big and expensive homes; thinking that when the home price will rise and they will be in profit.

The rate of foreclosure during the last quarter has passed the highest point recorded 54 years back in the year of 1953. The number of sub prime borrowers those who are currently behind on their home loans has increased to 14.82 percent. The homes that are purchased with 2/28 adjustable rate mortgages are under the highest percentage of foreclosure. The credit crunch is not only making mortgage financing tougher but also it also pushing more homeowners towards foreclosure.

According to most recent Mortgage Bankers Association's survey, the foreclosure crisis is likely to increase in the near future. Since during the last quarter, the foreclosure rates in states like California, Florida, Arizona, Indiana and in few other states almost touched the sky, so it is expected that the foreclosure problem will become worse in the coming period before it stabilizes again.

It is expected that the number of foreclosures and payback delinquencies will rise during this quarter and may be in the next quarter too. Since the mortgage interest rate is rising high once again due to the fall in the home prices, the act of refinancing has become more difficult for the current borrowers those who are not comfortable with their current interest rate and wants to refinance at some lower interest rate.

According to Mortgage Bankers Association, the main reasons behind the foreclosure crisis is the 2/28 adjustable rate mortgage and the economic condition that is under pressure. Most of the foreclosures in the mortgage market are the result of these adjustable rate mortgages that normally offers low introductory interest rates and when the rate adjusts after a few years, most of the homeowners find difficulty to meet their monthly payments. With more adjustable rate mortgage expected to reset this year and in the coming year, it is probable that the rate of foreclosure will also increase during that time.

Appendix Two:
State-Specific Resources

Again, the materials in the appendices are not drafted by the author. She is not an attorney in the states that are the subject of these articles, and makes no representations as to the law in these states. These articles are meant to be of general interest only and should only be used as a starting point for more fully informed research and consultation.

Florida Foreclosure Proceedings

The following article details the final court proceedings for foreclosure cases in the state of Florida. The article details the different scenarios that can occur to finalize a foreclosure case. It is important for people facing foreclosure in the state of Florida to be aware of their rights so that they can do everything in their power to stop foreclosure through legal remedies.

The right to be heard at the hearing to show cause is waived if the defendant, after being served as provided by law with an order to show cause, engages in conduct that clearly shows that the defendant has relinquished the right to be heard on that order. The defendant's failure to file defenses by a motion or by a sworn or verified answer or to appear at the hearing presumptively constitutes conduct that clearly shows that the defendant has relinquished the right to be heard.

If the court finds that the defendant has waived the right to be heard, the court may promptly enter an order requiring payment in the amount provided or an order to vacate the premises. An order to vacate the premises is delivered to the County Sheriff for eviction should the mortgagor continue to occupy the premises.

If the court finds that the mortgagor has not waived the right to be heard on the order to show cause, the court will, at the hearing on the order to show cause, consider the affidavits and other showings made by the parties appearing and make a determination of the probable validity of the underlying claim alleged against the mortgagor and the mortgagor's defenses. If the court determines that the mortgagee is likely to prevail in the foreclosure action, the court will enter an order requiring the mortgagor to make the payment to the mortgagee and provide for a remedy. However, the order shall be stayed pending final adjudication of the claims of the parties if the mortgagor files with the court a written undertaking executed by a surety approved by the court in an amount equal to the unpaid balance of the mortgage on the property, including all principal, interest, unpaid taxes, and insurance premiums paid by the mortgagee.

In the event the court enters an order requiring the mortgagor to make payments to the mortgagee, payments shall be payable at such intervals and in such amounts provided for in the mortgage instrument before acceleration or maturity. The obligation to make payments pursuant to any order entered under this subsection shall commence from the date of the motion filed hereunder. The order shall be served upon the mortgagor no later than 20 days before the date specified for the first payment. The order may permit, but shall not require the mortgagee to take all appropriate steps to secure the premises during the foreclosure action.

In the event the court enters an order requiring payments the order shall also provide that the mortgagee shall be entitled to possession of the premises upon the failure of the mortgagor to make the payment required in the order unless at the hearing on the order to show cause the court finds good cause to order some other method of enforcement of its order.

All amounts paid pursuant to this section shall be credited against the mortgage obligation in accordance with the terms of the loan documents, provided, however, that any payments made under this section will not constitute a cure of any default or a waiver or any other defense to the mortgage foreclosure action. Upon the filing of an affidavit with the clerk that the premises have not been vacated pursuant to the court order, the clerk shall issue to the sheriff a writ for possession that shall be governed by the provisions of Florida state laws.

It is important for people facing foreclosure to understand their rights and to take the proper steps to ensure these rights are protected. It is very possible that one can stop foreclosure on their property by utilizing the methods lenders provide to address their situation.

California Foreclosure Proceedings

The California home-buying process usually involves the use of the deed of trust, which by its legal definition involves three parties; the trustor (borrower), the beneficiary (lender), and the trustee (neutral third party receiving the right to foreclose). The deed of trust usually includes a power of sale clause that gives the trustee the legal right to enforce collection of the debt. Collection of the debt is ultimately enforced by the right to sell the house when the borrower fails to make their mortgage payments.

Defaulting on one's loan causes the start of foreclosure, the process by which the lender takes over the home in order to recover his principal investment. Once the house is either sold at auction or "repossessed" by the lender, it is sold and the former owner must vacate at the discretion of the new owner. When there is a power of sale clause in the deed of trust, the non-judicial process of foreclosure is used. In non-judicial foreclosure the trustee must meet a few requirements before he or she sells the property. In comparison to a judicial foreclosure, non-judicial foreclosure is quick because the trustee does not have to obtain a court order to foreclose, nor is court supervision required in order to sell the house, as is required in the judicial foreclosure process. The judicial process of foreclosure is used when a power of sale clause is not in the deed of trust.

In California, the timeline of non-judicial foreclosure begins when the trustee files a notice of default. This is a letter that is sent to the owner/trustor notifying him or her of their default of the loan. This notifies the owner of the intent of the lender to follow through on their right to collect on the debt. The copy of the notice, which is recorded at the County Recorders Office of the appropriate county, is mailed to the address of notice as per the deed of trust. Recording of the notice of default can vary greatly depending on the beneficiary. In can occur anywhere between a week to many months after one misses their first mortgage payment.

The step that follows next is that stage of the foreclosure process in which there is a filing of the Notice of Trustee's Sale. No sooner than ninety (90) days after the trustee records the notice of default, the Trustee must publish a notice of trustee's sale in the local paper and simultaneously file that notice with the county recorder's office. No sooner than twenty days (20) after the notice of trustee sale is filed, the home may be sold at public auction for the amount of the debt plus foreclosure costs. If no one bids at the auction, the lender assumes ownership of the property, and may dispose of that property to recover his or her cash investment.

Appendix Three:
Foreclosure Issue Spotting Checklist

This is very similar to the checklist that we use in my law firm when analyzing incoming foreclosure cases. It is meant to clue the reviewer in on the large variety of potential defenses that may exist in a judicial foreclosure case. The author designed this checklist and has found it a tremendously helpful tool in analyzing foreclosure cases. There's just too much to keep in one's mind when reviewing a foreclosure file; it's a complicated subject. A checklist like this one really helps. We prefer to print out a copy and write our notes in by hand, highlighting things in one color that we need to follow up on for more information and in a second color that we think might form the basis for a defense or claim.

INITIAL ISSUES

- [ ] Was borrower advised of default and right to cure?
- [ ] When does the right to cure expire?
- [ ] Was the amount to cure default correctly calculated?
- [ ] Was borrower duly served with complaint?
- [ ] All necessary docs attached to complaint?
- [ ] Are there any unsatisfied requirements for out of state defendants?
- [ ] Is lender licensed in state? Was it at loan issuance?
- [ ] Is the plaintiff seeking a deficiency judgment?
- [ ] What is the anticipated redemption period?
- [ ] Is property a homestead? Could/can it be split?
- [ ] Does the loan contract require the lender consider alternatives to foreclosure? Did it?
- [ ] Were any mediation notice requirements followed?
- [ ] Is mortgage/loan notarized? Meet reqs for recording?
- [ ] Check dates on all loan docs
- [ ] Read legal descriptions and compare to parcel map and tax ID numbers, on mortgage/note and complaint
- [ ] Has a letter report been obtained? Should one be?

FAILURE TO JOIN INDISPENSABLE PARTIES

- [ ] What other entities have an interest?
  - o Who is named on note?
  - o Who is named on mortgage?

- o Anyone gotten married since loan issued?
- [ ] Were they all named in action?
- [ ] Who is living in the home? Are they named?
- [ ] Is there evidence that all past interests are extinguished?
- [ ] If the plaintiff is the servicer, is note holder named?

STANDING

- [ ] Who is plaintiff? What's its interest/role vis-à-vis loan?
- [ ] Does plaintiff have contractual right to enforce note?
- [ ] If plaintiff is servicer, does it demonstrate it has the right to enforce note, not the owner?
- [ ] If plaintiff is servicer, what is state view on right to enforce note for servicers?
- [ ] Did it at time of filing complaint?
- [ ] Does plaintiff have property interest in the real estate?
- [ ] Check MERS system to see if property listed (tinyurl.com/merscheck)?
- [ ] Doubt on existence of original note? Demand original?
- [ ] Critically examine allonges
- [ ] Critically examine assignments
- [ ] Request an accounting for pay off amount
- [ ] Any class action against plaintiff or past note holders?
- [ ] How did current owner come to own note?
- [ ] Does note identify current owner as payee?
- [ ] Do assignments show clear chain of ownership?

☐ Does the plaintiff have a federal license?
www.nmlsconsumeraccess.org
☐ Failed banks or rcvrs?
tinyurl.com/failedbanksearch

ACCOUNTING

☐ Was borrower in default?
☐ Does borrower agree the accounting is accurate?
☐ Were any inspections authorized or necessary?
☐ Are all charges/fees authorized under loan agreement?
☐ Is there any forced place insurance?
☐ Was the interest correctly calculated?
☐ Have all payments been credited? For trial loan mods?
☐ Are there any duplicative charges?

WAIVER, LACHES, AND SOL

☐ Any pattern to support borrower's reasonableness?
☐ When did borrower go into default?
☐ What was statute of limitations on default claim?
☐ Did lender wait unreasonable amount of time to file?
☐ Any promises to the plaintiff that weren't fulfilled?
☐ Did borrowers successfully complete a trial period loan mod?

PREDATORY LENDING

- [ ] How was the loan initiated?
- [ ] What is the interest rate on the loan?
- [ ] Is there a balloon payment on the loan?
- [ ] Did loan set the borrowers up to fail?
- [ ] All material terms of the loan disclosed to buyers?
- [ ] Any misrepresentation?
- [ ] Any terms that seem abusive in loan?
- [ ] Were closing costs unreasonably high?
- [ ] Did the loan shift unsecured debt into mortgage debt?
- [ ] Was the loan in excess of 100% loan to value?
- [ ] What were the monthly payments?

FEDERAL CLAIMS AND DEFENSES

- [ ] Was this a HAMP loan (tinyurl.com/hamplookup)?
- [ ] Were borrowers given chance to apply for HAMP mod?
- [ ] Did borrowers apply for a HAMP mod?
- [ ] Was their application properly handled?
- [ ] Potential for or attempt at TILA rescission?
- [ ] Any FDCPA issues? Contact at work? Harassment?
- [ ] FDCPA notifications provided? Collector identified?
  - o Provided verification of debt on request?
  - o Right to dispute debt mentioned?
- [ ] Any borrower in active military w/i 9 months?

BANKRUPTCY ISSUES

- [ ] Has the borrower gone through bankruptcy?
- [ ] When, in relation to the loan, was the bankruptcy?
- [ ] If after, what was the impact on the loan?
- [ ] Was there an exclusion for the loan?
- [ ] Are borrowers candidates for personal bankruptcy?
  - What is their debt load?
  - What kind of income do they have?
  - Would a restructuring be manageable?
  - Potentially unsecured second mortgage?

JUDGMENT ISSUES

- [ ] When was lis pendens filed? v. When judgment issued?
- [ ] Has plaintiff fulfilled burden to prove standing?
- [ ] Has plaintiff put evidence of interest in note on record?
- [ ] Has P put evidence of interest in property on record?
- [ ] Has copy of note been authenticated?
- [ ] Does person on affidavit have personal knowledge?
- [ ] Does affidavit meet procedural reqs for admission?
- [ ] Where defendants given a chance to defend? I.e., served and given time? A hearing?

FORECLOSURE SALE

- [ ] Was notice published?
- [ ] Was borrower served?
- [ ] Were tenants served?

- ☐ How many bidders at sale?
- ☐ What was value of home? Assessed? Zillow?
- ☐ What percentage of value did home sell for?
- ☐ Is this percentage reflect in the range of fair value?
- ☐ Were reqs for homestead foreclosure followed?

FORECLOSURE DEFENSE
LITIGATION TRACKSHEET

We use something close to the following checklist in order to track of the status of each of our Wisconsin foreclosure defense cases, and we continually update the checklist as the case progresses.

CASE NAME: _____

CASE NUMBER: _____

COUNTY: _____

BANK LAWYER: _____

Responsive Pleading

- [ ] Determine deadline to respond (20 days from service): _____
- [ ] Perform preliminary review of case using foreclosure checklist
- [ ] File a motion to dismiss or determine no valid grounds
- [ ] File an answer (within 10 days of denial of motion to dismiss, if appropriate)
  - [ ] If client has already answered, include motion to amend *if* more than 6 months since service has passed (see § 802.09)
  - [ ] If deadline has passed, include motion to enlarge time

Request Mediation, Pay-Off, Reinstatement

- [ ] Request within 30 days of service
  - [ ] Mediation request forms available at http://tinyurl.com/lhvumoy
- [ ] Request Pay-Off Amount
- [ ] Request Reinstatement Amount

Thoroughly Review ALF Foreclosure Checklist

- [ ] Discuss case with client, answer all questions on checklist

Discovery

☐ Draft and serve discovery on Plaintiff and any
other desired parties
  ☐ Tickle deadline to respond (30 days from
  service): _____
  ☐ Responses received?
  ☐ Responses carefully reviewed?
☐ Discovery propounded on client by bank
  ☐ Calculate deadline to respond (30 days):
  _____

  ☐ Responses served?

Post-Discovery

☐ Revisit ALF Foreclosure Checklist to see if any
new issues arose
☐ Review to see if answer should be amended
☐ Evaluate whether any dispositive motions are
possible

LAST UPDATED: _____

About the Author

Kimberly Alderman is an attorney who has practiced law in several states. She has focused her practice primarily on litigation consulting and appeals, but fell into foreclosure practice rather by accident. In Alderman's early efforts to educate herself on foreclosure defense, she found that the market was lacking in materials for an audience who sought a meaningful understanding of foreclosure, but who lacked pre-existing experience with foreclosure defense. Accordingly, when she earned a broader understanding of the practice, Alderman sought to write the book that she had been looking for at the beginning. She hopes you have found *Foreclosure Defense: Litigation Strategies and Appeals* an introduction to the topic worthy of your time.

www.ingramcontent.com/pod-product-compliance
Lightning Source LLC
Chambersburg PA
CBHW020203200326
41521CB00005BA/234